TO BE A
MILITARY SNIPER

Gregory Mast and Hans Halberstadt

ZENITH
PRESS

First published in 2007 by Zenith Press, an imprint of MBI Publishing Company LLC, Galtier Plaza, Suite 200, 380 Jackson Street, St. Paul, MN 55101 USA

Zenith Press titles are also available at discounts in bulk quantity for industrial or sales-promotional use. For details write to Special Sales Manager at MBI Publishing Company, Galtier Plaza, Suite 200, 380 Jackson Street, St. Paul, MN 55101 USA.

To find out more about our books, join us online at www.zenithpress.com.

About the Authors

Gregory Mast enlisted in the Marine Corps in 1978 and was commissioned in 1983. Following his active military service he worked in the defense industry on classified projects, as a web communications specialist at design studios, and as a freelance graphic designer, and he has owned a traditional Irish pub. He and his wife live in San Jose, California.

Hans Halberstadt studied documentary film in college and later took up writing, authoring or co-authoring more than fifty books. Most of his books have been on military subjects, especially U.S. special operations forces, armor, and artillery. He has also written extensively about farming and railroads. Halberstadt served in the U.S. Army as a helicopter door gunner in Vietnam. He and his wife, April, live in San Jose, California.

Unless otherwise noted, all photographs © Hans Halberstadt, militaryphoto.com.

Cover: Lance Corp. Juan Vella, sniper, 1st Battalion, 4th Marine Regiment, Regimental Combat Team 1 (RCT1), holds security with HN Clint Sprabary as his spotter in Al Shur, Iraq, March 24, 2003. *U.S. Marine Corps, Cpl. Mace M. Gratz*

Frontispiece: When snipers talk about "one shot, one kill," they are talking about shots made with M118LR ammunition. These 7.62mm NATO rounds use match-grade "boat-tail" open-tip bullets and are much more accurate than standard military ammunition. At about two dollars per cartridge, this ammunition is a battlefield bargain when compared to any other munition.

Title Page: Experienced instructors mentor students through target-detection exercises by experienced instructors. This civilian instructor has combat experience that dates back to the Vietnam war, and he is able to offer practical, real-world advice to his students, some of whom are young enough to be his grandson.

Table of Contents: Members of this team from the Special Operations Target Interdiction Course (SOTIC) have modified their rifles to attach to a photographer's tripod. SOTIC trains Green Beret, SEAL, and ranger snipers at Fort Bragg, North Carolina.

Back Cover, top left: Although the spotter can't normally see the actual bullet in flight, he can see the momentary disturbance of the air as it passes, a phenomenon called "trace." He can also see the impact of the bullet on some targets—a puff of dust from a hit on the ground or a masonry wall, and a pink cloud of blood and tissue with some hits on human targets. **Top right:** A U.S. Marine attached to 1st Battalion, 8th Marine Regiment, 1st Marine Division, looks for insurgent activity in Fallujah, Iraq, November 10, 2004, during Operation Al Fajr. *USMC, Lance Cpl. Trevor R. Gift* **Bottom right:** A sniper's-eye view of beautiful, scenic, uptown Ramadi. This is typical of many areas of urban Iraq, with many abandoned cars, trash, and clutter—excellent places for hiding bombs or preparing ambushes. *Harry Martinez, Shadow Team*

Library of Congress Cataloging-in-Publication Data

Mast, Gregory.
  To be a military sniper / by Gregory Mast ; photography by Hans Halberstadt.
    p. cm.
  ISBN 978-0-7603-3002-9 (softbound)
  1. Sniping (Military science) 2. Snipers—United States. 3. Fort Benning (Ga.) I. Title.
  UD333.M315 2007
  356'.162—dc22

                            2007027326

Editor: Steve Gansen
Designer: Jenny Bergstrom

Printed in China

CONTENTS

Acknowledgments

This book attempts to tell a small part of a very complex story, the story of how an ordinary soldier or marine learns an extraordinary set of skills and joins the often misunderstood brotherhood of snipers. It is a big story and this is a small book, one that could not be written without the assistance and encouragement of many people. I am deeply grateful and indebted to everyone who helped me put this project to bed, but there are some who deserve special recognition.

In a break with tradition I will acknowledge my wife, Vernie, first and foremost. The author's spouse is usually relegated to the "and finally" paragraph of the acknowledgements. Vernie tolerated not only my extended research trips, nearly two months at Fort Benning for a sniper competition and sniper school, but my maniacal behavior as the deadline loomed. Some writers manage to complete their books with erudite calm. I'm not one of those guys but Vernie still loves me anyway. This book was completed during a time of great personal difficulty for Vernie, as her mother passed away shortly after my return from sniper school. Her mother, Ruth, followed my literary antics with interest and I think it only fair that she receive a posthumous dedication as well.

My co-author, Hans Halberstadt, deserves some extra applause. He stepped in and lent extra assistance during some very trying times as this book was being rushed to completion. Thanks, Hans!

This was my second project at Fort Benning. Anyone familiar with military writing knows that the Public Affairs Office (PAO) can make or break a project. This book would simply not be possible were it not for the support of the Fort Benning PAO. They were extremely helpful in accommodating my request to observe the operations at Benning, and the instructors and cadre of the sniper school went out of their way to make sure that the time I spent at Harmony Church was not wasted.

Without their help this book would not be possible and a few lines of acknowledgement at the front of this book hardly seem adequate to express my appreciation. Elsie Jackson graciously coordinated my visits and gave me the official stamp of approval that allowed me to hang out with the guys at Harmony Church. Thanks, Elsie!

The PAO gave me access but the U.S. Army Sniper School (USASS) gave me the story. I do not know if I have the words to adequately express my gratitude to the school cadre for the generous assistance and extreme tolerance that was their gift to me while I was observing their operations. They work under a grinding, relentless training schedule driven by the demands of an army at war, day in and day out, trying to cram as much information as possible into the students during the five weeks they have them at Harmony Church. It takes a special blend of professional knowledge, personal resolve, and, above all, a sense of humor to take on this difficult task. Civilian contractors, all of whom are retired soldiers, augment the active-duty instructors. The contractors bring a depth of experience that is not only impressive but also invaluable. The colorful characters who populate the instructional staff at USASS are worthy of their own book. Operational security prevents me from naming them individually, but they know who they are. Keep in touch and I will make sure that you get an autographed copy of the book.

In the end, these acknowledgements would not be complete without thanking the class of students I observed and, occasionally, participated along with. To the twenty-three students who graduated from Class 02-07 (Zero Two Zero Seven), I wish you the best of luck and safe returns. Remember, it pays to be a winner. Finally, special thanks goes to Staff Sgt. David Piggot who took a chance by letting an old guy be his sniper buddy on Record Fire 4.

Preface

Two hours after dawn and the day is already getting hot. The mirage shimmers and moves with the wind as you watch a teenager with an AK-47 through your scope. You estimated his range at 480 meters, based on the length of his rifle. He is guarding the rural compound with resigned boredom, sitting on the ground with his back resting against the mud wall in a bit of shade near the gate. He's not much younger than you, maybe your brother's age you guess, and what he doesn't know is that today is his lucky day because he is not your target.

You would be a bit bored too if you weren't so deep in Indian Country with just your observer and a radio for backup. There should be at least four on this mission but your battalion has too many missions and too few shooters. So you and your observer are extra careful to not draw unwanted attention to your position, where you've been since late yesterday. You infiltrated the target area as dusk was settling, close enough to get a good shot but far enough away in case you need to call in artillery or close air support on the target.

Intel said that there would be about a squad in the compound and so far you've counted fourteen fighters. You and your observer take turns watching the compound, hoping that they are careless about patrolling. You try to catch a few minutes of sleep here and there, but your buddy kicks you awake when you start snoring and the dream gets good. He always does that and you start to concoct another prank you will play on him back inside the wire. You know him as well as you've ever known anybody and the two of you literally trust each other with your lives.

A reliable source told Intel that a local militia leader would be visiting the compound sometime today and your mission is to promote him to Martyr First Class if he shows up. You and your buddy joke about what it takes to be considered "reliable," actual information or just a blood pressure and body temperature that approaches normal. You hope that they are right this time because you've got a good position and what appears to be a safe, covered route to the extraction point. On the other hand, you've been on many other missions that were a bust because the reliable source wasn't reliable.

Several hours later you notice that a table is being set up in the shade of the courtyard. From your hillside position, you can look down into most of the walled compound and it would be a stroke of luck if this supposed meeting took place outside. Your first plan was to shoot as the target left his vehicle and walked to the building. You are keeping track of the environmental conditions that will affect your firing solution, such as the wind speed and direction, temperature and humidity. You and your observer have both estimated the ranges in the compound and have taken into account the downward angle that you will be firing from. You are keeping track of the temperature of your ammunition and if you were Tom Berenger you would be filing down your fingertip. You and your buddy like to make fun of cheesy sniper movies and will ask each other the rhetorical question, "What would Tom do?" to get a laugh.

Another couple of hours go by and your observer spots a pair of old Mercedes driving up to the compound. The cars stop at the gate and six armed men get out. Bingo, your target is there. They are met by the goobers that you've been watching all day and you wonder if the militia leader knows how lazy these guys are. After a few hugs and kisses they go inside and take seats at the table in the courtyard.

Damn, if they had shown up an hour earlier the light would have been perfect. Your observer is estimating the wind as you slowly chamber a round into your rifle. You dial in the windage and distance into your scope and take aim. He's too far away to risk a head shot so you will send the bullet crashing through his chest instead. It won't be an instant kill but it will certainly wreck his day. As you place the cross hair reticle on the target, you adjust your point of aim based on your knowledge of how this rifle shoots when the barrel is cold.

"Spotter ready" your observer tells you, letting you know that he has the target acquired in his spotting

On March 27, 2003, a sniper assigned to A Company, 2/505 Parachute Infantry Regiment, 82nd Airborne Division, provides security while the unit searches for a large cache of weapons in the Kohi Sofi region of Afghanistan. He's equipped with a modified version of the old, not very accurate, M14 rifle. *U.S. Army, Sgt. 1st Class Milton H. Robinson*

A U.S. Marine shoots an M107 .50-caliber Barrett sniper rifle at vehicle targets during a live-fire exercise at the Godoria Range in Djibouti's northern training area, August 26, 2006. The M107 is just one of the tools of the trade for modern snipers, the weapon of choice for killing trucks or light-skinned vehicles at ranges up to a mile. *Department of Defense, Staff Sgt. Reynaldo Ramon, U.S. Air Force*

A U.S. Army sniper team from Jalalabad Provincial Reconstruction Team (PRT) scans the horizon after reports of suspicious activity along the hilltops near Dur Baba, Afghanistan. Snipers work in pairs, a shooter and a spotter. *U.S. Army, Cpl. Bertha Flores*

scope. You take a few deep breaths to calm down and tell him, "Shooter ready." When he says "Send it!" you gently squeeze the trigger and dispatch a 175-grain greeting card downrange. You lose sight of your target as the rifle recoils, giving your shoulder a familiar shove. Your observer watches the bullet's "trace," the projectile's supersonic atmospheric wake that marks its path to the target. After the rifle recoils, you slowly manipulate the bolt and chamber another round in case you need to re-engage the target.

It won't be necessary this time. Your observer watched the round impact into the target's chest and could see his brief expression of surprise before he fell over backward in his chair. The report of the rifle arrives a split second after the bullet and in the confusion the fighters shoot wildly into the hills, some of their fire directed vaguely toward your hidden position. You are watching to see if they are going to start searching for you or just hole up inside the compound, getting under cover to avoid more casualties. While you are watching and packing your gear for a swift exit, your observer is on the radio giving a mission update and requesting an extraction. He will also prep a fire mission if it looks like you are going to be chased.

It will be totally dark in a few hours but you decide to leave now, while the home team is still confused. You and your observer quickly put distance between you and the compound, stopping occasionally to see if you are being followed. Four hours later you are inside a Black-hawk, hoping the pilot is really good with night-vision goggles and that he knows where all the power lines are in this area. Once you are back on friendly turf, you will be debriefed on the mission before you can clean up and get chow. After that, you catch a bit of sleep and it all starts over the next day. Another day, another mission.

The author as a USMC lance corporal at Camp Pendleton, California, in 1980. He was a member of the Surveillance and Target Acquisition platoon for 1st Battalion, 23rd Marines. *Gregory Mast*

This scenario is a composite of many different missions, but it illustrates some of the skills and mindset that a military sniper must have in order to survive on the modern battlefield. This book intends to offer an introduction to what it takes to become a sniper in today's armed forces, a specialty known for its economical motto of "one shot, one kill." It is not a story for the squeamish because the brutal reality of the sniper's trade is the delivery of death, one shot at a time. It is a story that even many military professionals know little about, and it is a story where the reality is much more interesting than the fantasy. The first step is to meet those who have made the grade and work as snipers.

A sniper team from the 10th Mountain Division shares a joke during the Sixth Annual International Sniper Competition hosted by the U.S. Army. They are each wearing a "ghillie suit," a camouflaged garment whose design and construction varies quite a bit. Generally, the foundation is an old set of BDUs that have been reinforced with heavier fabric on heavy-wear areas—elbows, knees, and chest. The front of the suit is typically kept bare to reduce weight and make crawling easier. This sniper's M24 is equipped with the PVS-10, a fixed-power day/night sight.

Typical sniping missions today are done mostly in urban areas and from hides in industrial and residential buildings. These missions present a special set of challenges and opportunities quite different from the traditional mission in rural terrain. *Harry Martinez, Shadow Team*

Introduction

Few other military specialties are as shrouded in mythology and misinformation as are snipers. The dominant popular image of the military sniper is that of a solitary hunter, stalking his prey with stealth and patience, shooting from such a long distance that the bullet arrives at the target long before the report of the shot. One rifle, one target, one shot, one kill. Often these tales are embellished with improbable details of near supernatural abilities and are fueled by the ballistically impossible cinematic exploits of Hollywood. While the basis of this image is not necessarily incorrect, that of a superbly trained marksmen delivering precision fire on high-value targets, the reality of modern warfare and conflict creates a story far more complex and interesting than any cheesy action movie.

When properly employed, the sniper is the smartest weapon on a battlefield dominated by "smart" weapons. For nearly two hundred years the sniper has been hated and revered, feared and admired, demonized and idealized, opinions dictated by one's relative position to the sniper's rifle. The modern sniper is carefully selected, rigorously trained, and specially equipped for his deadly tasks; and his leaders are educated on how to use this highly specialized asset. This process has many "moving parts" and, when done correctly, produces results far out of proportion to the size of the effort. The story of how an ordinary trigger puller becomes a sniper is a fascinating one; and it's a story that is seldom told.

The first stage in this process is the selection of candidates for sniper training. The simple fact is that many soldiers and marines are not suitable candidates for this line of work. Physical training (PT) scores and range qualifications alone do not a sniper make, although physical endurance and marksmanship skills are absolutely necessary. The basic candidate must possess above average intelligence, emotional maturity,

and a stable personality. Good judgment is a critical survival skill for snipers, who need to know when to shoot and when to scoot. Psychopaths and nutcases need not apply and are screened out by mandatory psychological exams. The candidate should also be a superior "field" soldier, knowledgeable in a wide range of military skills outside his own MOS.

The second stage is initial formal training, above and beyond preparatory training received at the unit level. This school can last anywhere from three to ten weeks, depending on the service component. During this training, the soldier or marine receives instruction in the basic skills of a modern sniper, traditional methodology that is constantly adapting to the changing battlegrounds of the twenty-first century. The course of instruction is rigorous and intense, with high attrition rates. The primary purpose of these schools is to train new snipers, the secondary purpose is to screen out unsuitable candidates.

The third stage of this process begins when the new sniper leaves school and ends when he is no longer a sniper. This is the real-world phase, where the sniper must maintain and perfect basic skills and constantly learn new tricks. Just as a shark must keep swimming to avoid drowning, so must a sniper train constantly for a battlefield where success and survival are often the same thing. Sometimes the schoolhouse solution works, sometimes it doesn't, but it is the experienced sniper who knows the difference. The sniper must also train those responsible for his employment, so that the employers understand the true operational capabilities and limitations of this highly specialized tool.

The modern sniper may be a direct descendent of sharpshooters past but he is as technologically removed from his ancestors as the B2 bomber is from the Wright brothers' first biplane. High technology and advances in the ballistic sciences have given the sniper capabilities

Opposite: Instructors from the U.S. Army Sniper School demonstrate stalking techniques. Even in an age of urban warfare, modern military snipers must be proficient in the traditional fieldcraft skills of hunting: the image of a sniper pursuing his prey, silently and relentlessly.

that were the stuff of science fiction less than thirty years ago. Still, it is the man behind the tool that makes the difference, not the tool. Like snipers in previous wars, the modern sniper lives and dies by his wits and skills, constantly searching for a better optics/bullet/rifle combination that will allow him to shoot farther, quicker, and more accurately than his opponent. In this, the sniper strives to live out the singular motto of those who went before him: one shot, one kill.

The term *sniper* conjures many images, most of them incorrect because the term is widely misused. A rifleman who makes a lucky long-distance shot is not a sniper nor is a deranged solitary gunman shooting from a rooftop. For the purpose of this book, a sniper is a highly trained, specially equipped and tasked service member who has a primary mission of delivering precision rifle fire on selected, high-value targets and a secondary mission of gathering battlefield information through observation and reporting. Every branch of the U.S. military employs snipers, both in conventional warfare and special operations roles. The overwhelming majority of those trained as snipers are in the army and Marine Corps but the air force and navy also have snipers in their special operations forces.

Snipers have made their mark in every war since the American Revolution. They have commanded fear or respect, depending which side of his rifle you were on. This marine was killed by intense Japanese sniper fire as he advanced on Iwo Jima on February 19, 1945. *Sgt. Bob Cooke, Marine Corps*

The modern military sniper must learn to deliver accurate fire from almost anywhere, including airborne platforms. This sniper is competing in the U.S. Army's Sixth Annual International Sniper Competition, firing at targets from a hovering Blackhawk helicopter. *Gregory Mast*

A sniper team from the army's 25th Infantry Division wait their turn to begin the stalk-and-shoot event at the Sixth Annual International Sniper Competition.

There are probably three to four thousand men assigned to sniper duties at any given time in the U.S. Armed Forces, a small number in the big scheme of things. Each service treats the craft differently, with the Marine Corps and army representing two basic approaches to career management for snipers. Snipers in the Marine Corps are assigned a Military Occupational Specialty (MOS), 8541, which makes sniping their primary duty. As a result, snipers in the Marine Corps have a defined career path. The U.S. Army assigns trained snipers an additional skill identifier (ASI) of B4, which is attached to their MOS. This approach may allow the army more flexibility in assigning soldiers but the "trade off" seems to be a diminished institutional value placed on sniping as a unique specialty.

The sniper tab is not an authorized item for the uniform, but it is often worn anyway as a distinction. Because the school graduates only a few hundred fully qualified "Bravo Four" snipers every year, this tab is rarely seen.

The total number of new snipers trained each year is not widely discussed but is estimated to range from four to six hundred. Initial sniper training is expensive, resource intensive, and time consuming, characteristics that are always unpopular with military bureaucracies, even more so during a time of war. The U.S. Army Sniper School at Fort Benning, Georgia, trains the largest

The modern battlefield demands that snipers be in excellent physical condition. The nature of their missions demands that they carry specialized equipment and lots of it. They must be able to run when needed while laden like a pack mule and road march any distance necessary to accomplish the mission. This Special Forces sniper team is dashing into position during the U.S. Army's Sixth Annual International Sniper Competition.

number of these new snipers, turning out nearly twice as many new shooters per year than the Marine Corps does. For that reason, the army sniper school was used as the example of a sniper training program for this book.

Snipers, by the nature of their work, have training and equipment requirements that set them apart from their peers. Snipers are employed in small teams, hidden from friend and foe alike, and operate in isolation and danger. Time is a precious commodity for an army at war and training for these complex missions must compete for time with the ordinary administrative requirements of military life. Any veteran of military service will remember the time-consuming paperwork necessary to keep a unit's books in order but that paperwork does nothing to improve combat skills. Snipers are selected for their intelligence, self-confidence, and ability to think creatively in order to accomplish their mission in the field, but these same attributes can

occasionally create friction in a garrison atmosphere of rigid military discipline. Snipers have developed an institutional reputation as star performers outside the wire and leadership challenges in the barracks.

"What makes snipers so special," one might ask, "if it is the mission of every combat unit to kill the enemy?" That's a fair question and one that is asked by many not familiar with the specialized skills, techniques, and equipment that make the sniper among the most efficient and cost-effective weapon on the battlefield. The sniper's efficiency as a weapon goes far beyond the box score of individuals who fall victim to his rifle. It is measured in the panic, chaos, and confusion he sows in the ranks of the enemy. A sniper's cost effectiveness is often expressed, somewhat simplistically, in the cost of his bullets of choice. While the bullet-per-kill model ignores the expense of training, the sniper and his team are incredibly

In quick-moving urban battles, snipers must be prepared to fire on targets of opportunity from nontraditional positions. This Airborne Ranger is engaging targets during the Sixth Annual International Sniper Competition, during a scenario that simulated situations encountered in Iraq.

cost effective when the results are measured against the relatively low costs of manpower and materials. What makes the sniper "special," however, is his primary mission—often couched in sanitized euphemisms so as not to shock polite society—which is the delivery of precision death, to specific targets from a concealed location.

Many soldiers and marines kill in the heat of battle. Sometimes they know who they've killed, more often than not they do not. The sniper's stock in trade is a deadly shot taken calmly, the details coolly calculated, and often after a lengthy observation of the target. The sniper almost always sees the face of his victim and sometimes can even place a name with the face. The sniper knows when he has taken a life and while many deal with this burden of knowledge differently none can deny their responsibility when they've squeezed the trigger and sent the bullet downrange. This is why emotional maturity and stable personalities are absolutely critical requirements during the selection of snipers. Any sniper with combat experience can remember every kill he made, much like the fighter pilots of World War II. This, in essence, is what makes the sniper "special": knowing the difference between when to shoot or not shoot and the ability to live with the consequences of that decision.

Above: Combining new technology and an old concept, the modern military sniper is the beneficiary of the technical and scientific advances of the past half century.

Left: Snipers must be well trained in a variety of weapons, especially their defensive side arms. This competitor in the Sixth Annual International Sniper Competition is engaging targets during a movement between positions.

ONE

Sergeant James "Rock" McGlynn, a marine scout/sniper in Beirut, Lebanon, in 1983, helped start the modern era of sniper tactics and employment doctrine during the wild period when multiple factions were fighting one another for control of Beirut. The locals often fired upon marines without fear of retribution, knowing that the snipers had to get permission before engaging targets. Nobody told them about the rule change until Sergeant McGlynn and a few other marines started killing the gunmen whenever they appeared. *U.S. Marine Corps/U.S. Department of Defense Archive*

A Brief History of Sniping

Colonel Hiram Berdan was a pivotal character in the history of sniping. A brilliant inventor and successful businessman, he raised and led two regiments of marksmen during the Civil War. The Berdan Sharpshooters were among the most successful units in the Union army.

Colorful characters, critical developments in technology, and the evolution of warfare define the history of sniping. Sniping may have its origins in the ancient art of hunting, but the collision of mass warfare and the Industrial Revolution created the modern sniper. The history of sniping is a fascinating story and far too complex to present comprehensively in this book. Highlights from history, however, can give some context to the sniper's role on the emerging battlefields of the twenty-first century and provide some understanding of the tradecraft.

THE AMERICAN REVOLUTION

The history of the sniper begins, in earnest, about the time of the American Revolution. During this time, skilled marksmen were first organized into specialized units, with the mission of delivering precise rifle fire on enemy soldiers. The standard musket in use by most armies was a smoothbore flintlock, which was an extremely inaccurate and short-range weapon. In order to deliver effective fire on enemy formations, infantry units equipped with these muskets would fire in unison (volley fire), often from ranges of less than 100 meters. The British army's standard issue long arm at the time of the American Revolution, the Land Pattern Musket—better known by the common nickname "Brown Bess"—was not even equipped with sights. The technology of the smoothbore musket dictated the tactics of mass formations engaging at short range, followed by a bayonet charge.

The concept of "rifling," cutting spiraled lands and grooves into a firearm's barrel to improve accuracy, was almost as old as the musket itself. Rifles, however, were not in common use in Europe because they were difficult to manufacture, considered too expensive for standard infantry issue, and required too much training to use. Also, the rate of fire for rifles was lower than smoothbores because the rifle's barrel had to be cleaned of

American snipers of the 166th Infantry (formerly 4th Infantry, Ohio National Guard) in a nest are picking off Germans on the outer edge of Villers sur Fere, France, July 30, 1918. The art and science of sniping was fully developed during World War I by both British and German forces, and the mission today is not significantly different than it was way back then.
U.S. Department of Defense/National Archives, Cpl. R. H. Ingleston,
www.historicmilitaryphotos.com

powder fouling after every shot. The long rifle, however, became something of an art form in the New World colonies of North America, where settlers' lives often depended on being able to hunt game or fight Natives. The American reputation for marksmanship was developed in the Alleghany and Appalachian mountains by colonists using the Kentucky rifle.

General David Morgan, cousin of the legendary Daniel Boone and one of the most gifted battlefield tacticians in the Continental army, was one of the first colorful characters to become associated with the development of sniping. In July 1775 he raised a company of marksmen that became known as Morgan's Riflemen, which he led with distinction during the disastrous invasion of Canada later that year. He was captured during the expedition against Quebec, led by Col. Benedict Arnold, and promoted to colonel after his release from captivity in January 1777. He was assigned to raise and lead a new regiment, the 11th Virginia Regiment, which he filled with four hundred of the finest marksmen he could find. Later that year, he made his mark in sniping history when he reluctantly ordered one of his men, Timothy Murphy, to shoot Gen. Simon Fraser during the Battle of Bemis Heights on October 7, 1777. General Fraser was rallying the British troops during the battle when Murphy's rifle mortally wounded him. Fraser was just one man but he was worth a regiment of troops and removing him from the battle was instrumental in the American victory.

Today, enemy officers are among a sniper's top priority of targets. In the late eighteenth century that sort of thing just wasn't considered sporting. Gentlemen simply did not shoot other gentlemen and the officers were drawn from the gentleman class. An anecdote that illustrates this attitude is the following story often referred to as the "Shot Not Taken." We will never know if this story is true but a single bullet from a single rifle on the banks of a creek in Pennsylvania could have changed the course of history.

Major Patrick Ferguson, a Scottish inventor, was a company commander in the 70th Regiment of Foot during the American Revolution. His namesake invention, the Ferguson rifle, was among the first breechloading rifles to be adopted into military service and was in use during the fateful Battle of Brandywine. On September 11, 1777, nearly eleven thousand Continental troops under the command of Gen. George Washington met a force of seventeen thousand British troops under the command of Gen. William Howe near Chadds Ford, Pennsylvania, in an engagement that would become known as the Battle

Marie Ljalková, shown here with an SVT-40, was a Czechoslovakian sniper who fought for the Soviet Union during World War II.

of Brandywine. During that battle, which was won by the British army, Major Ferguson is said to have taken aim at an obviously high-ranking American officer, but did not shoot him because he did not feel that it was right to shoot an officer in the back when he was conducting himself in such a calm manner under fire. It has been speculated that the officer in question was George Washington, whose death on that battlefield would have had greater consequences than merely the loss of the battle. Major Ferguson was badly wounded during this battle and was later killed in action at the Battle of Kings Mountain on October 7, 1780.

THE AMERICAN CIVIL WAR

Some historians have categorized the American Civil War as the first modern war. The Industrial Revolution of the early nineteenth century transformed the manufacturing capacity of a nation into a strategic military asset. Rapid advances were being made in science and engineering and many inventors became wealthy entrepreneurs, not unlike the phenomenon of Silicon Valley 125 years later. One such brilliant individual was Hiram Berdan, a prolific inventor, wealthy businessman, and superior marksman. Berdan's inventions included repeating rifles, improved musket balls, range finders, fuses for shrapnel shells, torpedo boats, and the first commercial gold amalgamation machine to separate gold from ore. These, and other inventions, brought him wealth and international acclaim. The rifles and primers that bear his name would have been enough to secure his place in military history, but it was his pioneering work in long-range shooting and tactical employment of specially trained and equipped marksmen that made him pivotal to the history of sniping.

For fifteen years before the start of the Civil War, Hiram Berdan was widely regarded as the best marksman in America, gaining this reputation in competitive target shooting. These competitions were a highly popular sport at the time and spurred the development of new technologies such as telescopic rifle sights. Berdan was a natural marksman and his knowledge of ballistics and long-range shooting were second to none when the South seceded from the Union. He recognized the value of organizing special units of marksmen, trained in long-distance shooting, to attack high-value targets such as enemy officers and artillerymen, and immediately began to lobby the president and the War Department to raise a regiment of sharpshooters.

Berdan was turned away repeatedly and he peddled his idea to anyone who would listen. Although Hiram Berdan was recognized for his brilliance, he was also immensely disliked. He had no military experience, yet he was seeking command of a regiment, and he had a personality that most believed made him unfit for command. He finally found a sponsor in Gen. Winfield Scott and in November 1861 he was given the rank of colonel and allowed to raise two regiments that would become known as Berdan's Sharpshooters. Berdan traveled throughout the states that remained loyal to the

Vasili Záitsev in Stalingrad, October 1942. He was popularized in the film *Enemy at the Gates*, a highly fictionalized account of his exploits during the Battle of Stalingrad.

Sergeant H. A. Marshall of the Calgary Highlanders, September 1944. Canadian snipers in the Second World War were also trained scouts. Specialized equipment includes his factory-tested No. 4 Mk I(T) rifle and scope combination and a camouflaged Denison smock. *Public Archives of Canada, Ken Bel*

union in order to recruit the best marksmen available, men who could place ten consecutive shots into a 10-inch circular target at a distance of 200 yards.

The 1st and 2nd U.S. Sharpshooters regiments were issued distinctive uniforms of forest green, instead of the standard army blue, and armed with repeating rifles that were outfitted with telescopic sights, a military first. Initially the regiments were issued Colt repeating rifles but soon exchanged them for the 1859 Sharps breechloader. During the three years that the regiments were in existence, they fought with distinction in numerous engagements, most notably at Gettysburg and Chancellorsville where the snipers under Berdan's command devastated enemy artillery units. Berdan's Sharpshooters are said to have killed more Confederates than any other unit in the Union army. Berdan left the army in 1864 after being wounded, and his regiments were disbanded shortly thereafter in 1865. Berdan felt that he was not given adequate recognition for his service and the army did eventually award him brevet promotions to brigadier general and major general in 1865. Hiram Berdan died in 1893 and is buried at Arlington National Cemetery.

The Confederate army started training and employing sharpshooters shortly after the Union allowed Berdan to form his regiments. They were, however, employed with the regular units rather than in specific units. They were mainly used as skirmishers and were often allowed to operate independently of their unit. Skirmishers would often seek out targets or just harass the enemy. They used an English rifle, the .45-caliber Whitworth, which had to be smuggled through the Union Naval Blockade. These rifles were a scarce commodity in the Confederate army and competition was fierce among the soldiers to become a sharpshooter. These soldiers were very skilled marksman but ultimately were not as effective as their Union counterparts due to their casual organization and employment.

WORLD WAR I

During World War I the term *sniper* came into common usage and gradually replaced *sharpshooter*. The term is believed to have its origin in the British army and dates to the late eighteenth century when British officers posted to India would hunt snipe, a wetland bird, for sport. It took skill and cunning to hunt these little birds, whose natural camouflage made them difficult to find and their speed on the wing made them elusive targets. Those who excelled at the sport were soon called *snipers* in recognition of their field craft and marksmanship.

Today, World War I is largely remembered for the trench warfare of the European front, wholesale slaughter of soldiers, and the intransigence of military bureaucracy in the face of change. Life in the trenches was filled with terrors but few were as feared as the enemy sniper and the single, deadly shot that was his signature. German snipers dominated the trenches early in the war. The British army soon learned to fear and respect this danger, often posting placards bearing a skull and crossbones and the warning "SNIPER" to mark vulnerable areas in the trenches. The early German advantage is often credited to the tradition of hunting, which was far more common among German soldiers than British soldiers. During WWI camouflage became an art form necessary to the survival of snipers because both sides pursued counter-sniper operations with intensity.

By the midpoint of the war, the German advantage in sniping was neutralized largely due to the efforts of Major Hesketh-Pritchard, who established the first sniper observation and scouting school for the British army. He operated under the guidelines that a candidate for sniper training must have a hunter's instinct, enduring patience, and acute powers of observation. He also stated that any man could be trained as a deadly shot with a telescopic sight, but that it took true dedication to become a sniper. Major Hesketh-Pritchard's assessments of the characteristics of a successful sniper are as valid today as they were in 1917.

A legacy of the sniper's deadly reputation lives on in the superstition that lighting more than three cigarettes with a single match will bring bad luck. This is believed to have originated in the trenches of France, where a match made an excellent aiming point for a sniper in the dark of night. Limiting a single match to three cigarettes was, in essence, a passive counter-sniper measure that became a force of habit for the soldiers and eventually a superstition.

WORLD WAR II

Rapid advances in military technology and doctrine marked the period between the world wars. As is often the case between wars, however, snipers and their craft were neglected, forgotten, eliminated, and sometimes just ignored. Among the major powers, only the Soviet Union maintained a large, well-trained sniper force during the 1930s. During this period the USSR made two notable contributions to sniping history. The Soviets were the first to deploy snipers in teams of two as a matter of doctrine. Prior to this time, snipers generally operated as lone individuals. The Red Army determined that a sniper was more likely to pull the trigger if he was part of a team and that having a spotter observe the shot increased the accuracy

Crowds of Parisians celebrating the entry of Allied troops into Paris scatter for cover as a sniper fires from a building on the Place de la Concorde on August 26, 1944. Although the Germans surrendered the city, small bands of snipers still remained. *Verna, Army, NARA FILE #: 111-SC-193008 War & Conflict Book # 1057 (Released to Public)*

Although Carlos Hathcock is certainly the most famous American sniper, with ninety-three confirmed kills, Sgt. Adlebert Waldron III had him beat with 109. Those kills were made in just five months, one at nine hundred yards with a single shot from a moving boat. He is using an M14 equipped with telescopic sight. *U.S. Department of Defense/National Archives, www.historicmilitaryphoto.com*

and efficiency of the operation. Western armies took some time to catch up to this concept, with the U.S. Army and Marine Corps employing solo snipers as late as the Vietnam War. The Soviets were also the first military force to train female snipers, many of whom were quite successful against the invading German army.

Once the war began, following Germany's invasion of Poland, both the German army and the British army reinstituted formal sniper training. By 1940, the British had established a sniper school at Bisley, with the Lovat Scouts providing much of the training. In Germany, the *Waffen SS* established a sniper training school at Zossen. As in World War I, the Germans had an early advantage in sniping, due to their superior field craft and specialized equipment. The motto for the German sniper at the time was "camouflage ten times, shoot once."

The U.S. Army had little or no formal training for its snipers during the war, although there was a very short course in advanced marksmanship established at Camp Perry, Ohio, for the duration. The U.S. Marine Corps relied on an informal training program for its scout snipers until a school was established at Camp Lejeune, North Carolina, in 1942.

World War II produced a number of snipers who became celebrities in their own time and legends of history due to their deadly success, recording hundreds upon hundreds of confirmed kills. In addition to their contributions to the tactical success of operations, they became fearsome psychological warfare weapons against the enemy. Rumors of their presence in an area of operation would create fear and uncertainty in the ranks, degrading a unit's morale and combat efficiency without having to fire a single bullet. Snipers also became propaganda tools to bolster the civilian morale on the home front and to provide motivation for soldiers of the same army. Some of the notable personalities included the following:

Simo Häyhä tops the list with 505 confirmed kills with his sniper rifle. Häyhä was a soldier in the Finnish army and made his name during the Winter War (1939–1940) between Finland and the Soviet Union. The Soviet Union invaded Finland and the vastly outnumbered Finns fought a brilliant and effective defensive campaign against the invaders. In addition to his five hundred plus kills with his rifle, Simo Häyhä is also credited with another two hundred from his submachinegun, all done during a period of one hundred days. He was wounded in action on March 6, 1940, and did not regain consciousness until March 13, the day peace was declared.

Captain Vasily Grigoryevich Zaytsev is probably the best-known sniper from World War II, largely due to the fictionalized film version of his exploits *Enemy at the Gates*. Zaytsev is officially credited with 242 confirmed kills, although some give him credit for up to four hundred. Of those kills, 225 were made during the Battle of Stalingrad.

The Soviet Union trained more than two thousand female snipers during World War II. One of them, Lyudmila Pavlichenko, is credited with 309 confirmed kills, 36 of which were enemy snipers. Lyudmila Pavlichenko, a history student at Kiev University when the war started, was wounded in action in 1942 and sent on a publicity tour of Canada and the United States while she was recovering. She is said to be the first Soviet citizen to be received by a U.S. president when she visited Franklin Roosevelt in the White House.

Matthäus Hetzenauer, a soldier in the 3rd Mountain Division, was the most prolific German sniper of the war, with 345 confirmed kills. Some lists may credit Erwin Konig with four hundred but he, along with a Heinz Thorvald (300), is believed to have been a fictional character that never existed. Private Hetzenauer was captured by the Red Army near the end of the war and spent five years in a Soviet prison camp.

KOREA TO PRESENT

Following World War II many countries, the United States included, once again shelved their sniper programs. The advent of hostilities on the Korean peninsula, and the many small wars fought in the latter half of the twentieth century, demonstrated that snipers would continue to play an important role on the modern battlefield. The U.S. Army and Marine Corps displayed what might be described as an institutionally indifferent approach to sniper training for thirty years after the end of World War II. During that time, through the end of

A U.S. Army sniper with Bravo Company, 502nd Infantry Regiment, 101st Airborne Division, stands ready to engage targets during a mission on the outskirts of Baghdad, Iraq, December 28, 2005. *Department of Defense, Spc. Lester Colley, U.S. Army (Released to Public)*

the Vietnam War, most sniper training, if it was conducted at all, was informal or conducted at division level schools. The U.S. Army opened its first centralized sniper school at Camp Perry, Ohio, in 1955 and promptly closed it in 1956.

The war in Vietnam established, again, that snipers require special training, equipment, and armaments if they are to be successful. The Marine Corps First Division established a sniper school in Da Nang in 1966, with scout sniper training also conducted at Camp Pendleton, California. The U.S. Army's first in-country sniper school was established in 1968 by the 9th Infantry Division, with several other divisions following suit later. The results of this training yielded immediate results with U.S. snipers reporting nearly 1,500 confirmed kills by late 1969. One measure of their success is an oft-repeated statistic that U.S. soldiers expended 200,000 rounds for every enemy KIA, compared to a sniper's average of 1.3 rounds for the same result.

The army and the Marine Corps took two different approaches to sniper rifles in Vietnam. The Marine Corps introduced the M40 sniper rifle in 1966, a bolt-action rifle based on the Remington M700. The U.S. Army modified an M14 rifle and designated it the M21. The most famous sniper of the war is undoubtedly Gunnery Sgt. Carlos Hathcock, with ninety-three confirmed kills to his credit. Gunny Hathcock was not the most prolific sniper in Vietnam, neither for the

Marine Corps or the army, but his story was immortalized in a bestselling book. The top honors go to U.S. Army sergeant Adelbert F. Waldron III who had 109 confirmed kills credited to him. Despite being awarded two Distinguished Service Crosses, the nation's second highest award for valor, for his heroic actions in Vietnam, he is largely unknown outside of the sniper community.

The U.S. Marine Corps centralized its sniper training at Quantico, Virginia, in 1977. Since then, the Marine Corps has set the standards for sniper training and doctrine at this world-famous facility. The U.S. Army opened their basic sniper school at Fort Benning, Georgia, in 1987. Although not as well known as the Marine Corps school, the army school graduates twice as many new snipers every year. The army and Marine Corps also conduct specialized sniper training at other locations, most notably the army's Special Operations Target Interdiction Course (SOTIC) held at Fort Bragg, North Carolina.

Since the mid-1980s the United States has developed a robust military sniper program. Snipers have been used in Lebanon, Panama, Haiti, Somalia, Bosnia, Iraq, and Afghanistan, as well as other locations. The technology snipers use is developing rapidly, driven by the demands of a global war on terror, and it is entirely likely that new equipment will have been introduced before this book is published.

TWO

The check-in process takes several hours. Students are briefed on the requirements of the course and the expectations of their performance. Their records and orders are checked and a gear inspection is conducted. This process is necessary because students still arrive at the school with incomplete paperwork or gear, despite the detailed instructions that are given to the students' command. *Gregory Mast*

Checking In

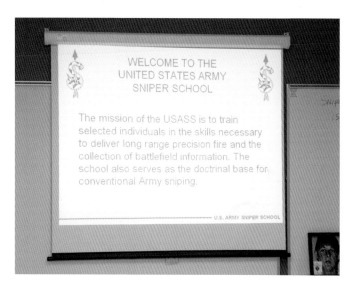

Welcome to Harmony Church, home of the U.S. Army Sniper School. Over the next five weeks, students will learn the basics of sniping. The course is both physically and mentally challenging. *Gregory Mast*

WELCOME TO HARMONY CHURCH
Snipers are made, not born, and this book is about that process. Although the army and Marine Corps have slightly different philosophies about the craft, they both impart similar skill sets on their new snipers. It should come as no surprise that there is intense inter-service rivalry between the Marine Corps and the army sniper community. The Marine Corps has the reputation of having the premier sniper training program and its basic sniper course is twice as long as the Fort Benning course. However, the army sniper school will provide the example of this process, for several reasons. Primarily, the basic skills and process of developing those skills are similar regardless of where a sniper is trained. The majority of all new snipers trained

Students muster in the courtyard in front of Building 4883, the USASS "head shed." The sniper school compound is located in an isolated part of Fort Benning, near the Ranger training brigade. *Gregory Mast*

by the United States are processed through the U.S. Army Sniper School (USASS).

The school is located at Fort Benning, Georgia. Fort Benning, a training and doctrine command (TRADOC) installation, is located just south of Columbus, Georgia. This huge installation is one of the busiest training commands in the army, hosting the U.S. Army Infantry and Airborne training programs and, in the near future, the U.S. Army Armor Center and School currently located at Fort Knox. Today, Fort Benning is home to the U.S. Army Infantry Training Brigade, U.S. Infantry School, Ranger Training Brigade, Airborne School, and the Western Hemisphere Institute for Security Cooperation (formerly known as the School of the Americas). It is also home to operational units, including the 3rd Brigade, 3rd Infantry Division (Mechanized), and the 75th Ranger Regiment headquarters and the 3rd Battalion, 75th Ranger Regiment, as well as combat support units.

U.S. Army Sniper School begins at 0500 on a crisp Monday morning with the standard Army Physical Fitness Test—a two-mile run, pushups, and situps. Be prepared to do the run in under 15:54 and do forty-three good pushups and seventy-three situps, or you'll be back on the bus and headed for your home station.

Fort Benning is a sprawling 182,000 acres of largely undeveloped, rolling and forested terrain; 93 percent of the base is in Georgia, the remaining 7 percent across the Chattahoochee River in Alabama. The compound that houses the Sniper School is located in Harmony Church, one of the four major cantonment areas at Benning. Harmony Church is relatively remote and also houses the Ranger Training Brigade and the 4th Ranger Training Battalion. The isolation of Harmony Church benefits both Ranger and sniper training programs. The sniper school instructors are identified by their black tee shirts or black jackets, emblazoned with the same symbol that

26

Class size is small, normally beginning with about thirty students. Week one includes more lectures and PowerPoint presentations than later weeks. Most of the instructors have combat experience, many as snipers, and all have been through the course themselves and know the material from personal experience.

adorns all army sniper documents and buildings, a rattlesnake coiled around an arrow forming an "S" shape.

The USASS basic sniper course is a physical and mental challenge, designed not only to train new snipers but to weed out those who are not suitable candidates. The course lasts a grueling five weeks, with more than five hundred hours of classroom instruction, physical training, practical field craft exercises, marksmanship training, evaluated evolutions, and equipment maintenance listed on the training schedule. Training is conducted six days a week, seven if weather or remedial instruction make it necessary. The curriculum is constantly updated to reflect lessons learned in combat during the ongoing war, but the basic skills snipers need such as range estimation, for example, remain constant and form the basis of the course of instruction.

The sergeants who make up the instructional staff are all experienced, "Bravo Four"–qualified professionals. Almost every instructor is a veteran of combat, many of them with combat time as a sniper. Civilian contractors, all of whom are retired or former soldiers with combat experience, augment the active-duty instructors. The contractors' combat experience date back to Vietnam and extend to the war in Iraq. This collective wealth of experience is apparent during instruction, where students are given the "school solution" with "real-world" examples. The combined cadre operate the school as a gentleman's

"Let me introduce you to the M24 sniper weapon system," the instructor says. The students will become extremely familiar with every detail of this weapon during week one.

The M24 is a simple weapon by modern standards, and extremely accurate. Snipers are expected to do all of the basic maintenance on the weapon, including disassembly of the bolt assembly and replacement of the firing pin and spring when necessary. These students are learning the tricks of bolt disassembly.

Students carefully examine the bolt's construction and function during one of the first classes on the weapon. The safety on all weapons is secured in the "safe" position during classroom training with rubber bands.

Another student tests the trigger function, studying the action of the sear where it normally engages the firing pin. The trigger is a critical component of the weapon, and proper function of this part, the students learn, is essential to accurate delivery of fire.

course, where "big boy" rules apply. This means that the students determine their own school experience by their behavior. Students are expected to conduct themselves as military professionals, and if they meet those expectations then sniper school is a difficult but enjoyable five weeks.

COURSE REQUIREMENTS

Candidates for sniper school must meet rigorous entrance requirements. In short, they must be physically and psychologically fit, have a consistent record of expert marksmanship scores, must be more intelligent than average, have a reputation for dependability and stability, have a clean disciplinary record, and be in an appropriate career management field. Unit commanders are responsible for conducting screening and ensuring that students arrive with required orders, records, and paperwork, along with a complete packing list. Although these requirements are explicit, some units still send students who are unqualified due to rank, MOS, or physical condition or allow students to arrive with incomplete or outdated records. Depending on the judgment of the school cadre, students who arrive unprepared may be

sent back to their units immediately or given a few days to have missing paperwork faxed to the school.

At the time of this writing, USASS course prerequisites were as follows:

Volunteer Status: All students must be volunteers. Students must have a letter of recommendation from either their battalion or regimental CO. This requirement may not be waived.

Rank: Students with ranks of Private First Class (E-3) through Sergeant First Class (E-7) are eligible to attend. All other ranks must obtain a waiver and approval to attend from the Course Convening Authority.

APFT: Students must achieve a minimum score of 70 percent in each event in the student's age group. The Army Physical Fitness Test (APFT) will be given on class start date. Participation is mandatory and this requirement may not be waived. Students more than forty years of age must have medical clearance for physical training. Students with medical or physical profiles will not be permitted to attend the course. An APFT will be administered during the check-in process and those students who do not achieve the minimum scores will be sent back to their unit of origin.

Physical Examination: Students must have a current physical examination dated within one year of the class start date. This requirement may not be waived.

Psychological Evaluation: Students must have an examination conducted by a qualified psychologist dated within six months of the class start date. This requirement may not be waived.

Career Management Field (CMF): The additional skill indicator (ASI) of B4 is available only to 11 series (infantry), 18 series (special forces), and 19D (cavalry scout) Military Occupational Specialties. This requirement may not be waived.

GT SCORE: Students must have a general technical (GT) score of 100 or higher to qualify for sniper training. This requirement may not be waived.

Weapons Qualification: Students must have a consistent track record of Expert qualification with the M16A1/M16A2 rifle or M4/M4A1 carbine. The most

recent qualification must be within six months of the class start date. This requirement may not be waived.

Retention: Students must have at least one year remaining on active duty from course end date. This requirement may not be waived.

Vision: Students must have a minimum of 20/200 correctable to 20/20. Color vision must be normal. This requirement may not be waived.

Discipline: Students must have no history of drug or alcohol abuse, nor any history of disciplinary actions. This requirement may not be waived.

Dependability: Students must be capable of working alone under adverse conditions for extended periods of time. This is a determination that unit commanders need to make when selecting candidates for sniper school.

All students must be in compliance with Army Regulation 600-9, the Army Weight Control Program.

Unit commanders are also provided with a detailed

On Wednesday of week one, the class is introduced to the complicated business of range estimation, first in the classroom, then on the well-manicured, thousand-meter Maertens Range. Students will carry their M24 rifles with them everywhere.

Each student is supplied with a clipboard and provides his own notebook and writing instruments, all of which will get a solid workout. The sniper mission requires more skill at mathematics and documentation than nearly any other military occupation.

Instructors and cadre begin a series of lessons on range estimation by demonstrating the appearance of objects at progressively longer distances. This man and truck are seven hundred meters from the students, and to the unaided eye, have become shapes without detail at this distance.

Meticulous note-taking is required to successfully complete the school. There is a tremendous amount of detail to absorb and to be able to repeat on both written and practical tests. This student is recording the variations in appearance of a person at various distances from one hundred meters to one thousand meters.

packing list for students. The list contains mandatory and optional items. *Optional* is a misleading term as the items identified as "optional" are critical non-issue items. Students may find that additional equipment, not listed, will also be useful during field craft training.

CURRICULUM OVERVIEW

From the time a student reports in at Building 4883 to the time he leaves the U.S. Army Sniper School, it is clear that this school experience is one of the most unique in the army. The school trains fewer than three hundred snipers a year, both from the resident course and from mobile training teams (MTT) after five intense weeks of training, making the graduates an elite group in an army of nearly one million soldiers. Each incoming class receives a briefing during the check-in process that outlines the course curriculum, performance standards, and a code of conduct. The cadre do not mince words and delicate egos are not coddled to protect self-esteem. The course is tough and only tough students eventually will graduate.

As noted earlier, the training schedule has five hundred hours allocated during the five weeks. Students who expect a forty-hour week are going to be sorely disappointed. Each training day begins around 0530 hours and often ends at 2100 hours or later. This demanding schedule requires an above average level of physical and mental stamina merely to keep up with the pace, much less excel. There seem to be two primary reasons for a schedule this tightly packed with activity. The first, and most obvious, is that five weeks is a very short amount of time to introduce soldiers to the very complex art of sniping. The second reason is that this allows instructors to observe students who are performing under the stress of fatigue and evaluate their judgment and maturity in the face of adverse conditions. Most soldiers can make good decisions when they are well rested, comfortable, and not under stress. Snipers must be able to make life or death decisions while operating under the stress of exhaustion, hunger, isolation, and physical discomfort.

In broad terms, the first week consists of equipment issue, classes on the basic skills to be developed during the course, introductory marksmanship training, and familiarization with the sniper rifle. The second week consists primarily of field craft training and advanced marksmanship training. The third week consists of stalking exercises, counter-sniper training, and moving-target marksmanship. The fourth week consists of urban operations, night marksmanship training, pistol marksmanship, and advanced ballistics topics. The fifth week consists of marksmanship training with the M107 long-range sniper rifle, a sniper culmination event, checking out, and graduation. Weather and base resource issues may dictate changes to the training schedule and the school cadre are adept at reordering the training as needed.

The primary reference document for sniper school is Field Manual 23-10 Sniper Training. At the time of this writing, the version in use (dated August 17, 1994) was widely considered to be outdated. The manual is under revision and is not available for public review. FM 23-10 will be quoted in this book as appropriate.

CHECKING IN

In-processing begins promptly at 0800 on the class report date. Students go through an extensive checklist during the in-briefing process, not only to check that all necessary paperwork is in order but also to ensure that students are qualified to attend the course. Statistical data is gathered on students such as combat service status or how much (if any) preparatory training a student received prior to reporting in at Harmony Church. This data is used to analyze trends in student performance and attrition rates. Checking in is normally conducted on a Sunday and takes about four hours. Included in this process is the student's first class, a short history of the modern sniper.

During the officer in charge's (OIC's) welcome brief, the first hour in school, students are introduced to the Honor Code. Integrity is a bedrock military principle and doing the right thing when no one is watching is a non-negotiable virtue at sniper school. Students who violate the Honor Code will be dropped from the course and may even receive non-judicial punishment under the Uniform Code of Military Justice. The Honor Code states:

> The Honor Code is based on the principle that integrity is an essential attribute of any soldier; therefore, any student found guilty of a breach of integrity will be relieved from the course, as well as face possible disciplinary action. The Honor Code while broad in application is precise in its meaning: "Each student's work is to be his own." No student may give or receive unauthorized aid. Any student who knows of an Honor Code violation, and fails to report it, has himself committed an Honor Code violation.

Students take the Army Physical Fitness Test the first morning of school. The minimum passing score in each event is 70 percent for the student's age group. For example, a 21-year-old student must complete 49 pushups, 59 situps in two minutes, and run two miles in 15 minutes 12 seconds or better to achieve a 70 percent score. The need for physical fitness cannot be over-emphasized. Snipers must be able to carry heavy packs for long distances and, regardless of what sidearm they carry, the sniper's primary defensive weapon is his ability to evade the enemy quickly. Being chased by angry locals is an occupational hazard that snipers must be prepared to encounter.

An instructor and his truck give the students a chance to study the appearance of common target objects at five hundred meters. The students are taught to use the unaided eye, the forty-power Leupold spotting scope, M22 binoculars, and, later, laser range finders.

One of the tricks students quickly learn is to use the sand sock on top of the rifle scope to provide a steady support for their binoculars. These binos have an internal scale, or reticle, that is calibrated in a way that permits the user to measure the dimensions of objects and calculate the distance to those objects.

THREE

The prone position is SOP for most practical demonstrations and classes, and the students line up in roster order. Each quickly learns that although the prone position may be comfortable, it frequently makes it more difficult to see and evaluate distant objects because of the "mirage" effect of warm air and because of sightline restrictions from weeds, grass, and brush.

Sniper Training: Week One

Many students will arrive with their own ghillie suits: some new commercial models, others home made at their old unit. Although ghillie suits are rarely used in real-world tactical operations today, making and using them provides important lessons about cover and concealment that apply to any operation.

OVERVIEW

In the first five days of sniper school, students are subjected to more than thirty hours of classroom academics. These classes address some, not all, of the fundamental skills a sniper must develop.

Learning to be a sniper means that you have to carry a lot of gear everywhere you go—rifle, spotting scope, binos, load-bearing vest or harness, ruck-sack with water, an MRE or two, notebook, clipboard, and helmet.

CLASSROOM INSTRUCTION

During the first week, students receive instruction in:

> Military sketch
> Sniper data book
> Range cards
> Keep-in-memory system (KIMS)
> Range estimation
> Ghillie suit construction
> Introduction to the M9 pistol
> Elevation and windage hold-off
> Practical exercises and field work
> Shooting and range work

MILITARY SKETCH

The secondary mission of snipers includes observation and reporting of battlefield information. Intelligence officers analyze information snipers gather and turn it into battlefield intelligence. Accurate intelligence requires accurate information from the source, and snipers must be able to relay that information. One tool for recording and transmitting the sniper's observations of his sector is a hand-drawn sketch. Sketches are valuable tools, even in this age of digital cameras, and students spend hours learning and practicing basic draftsmanship and drawing skills. Sketching forces the sniper to carefully observe his

sector and allows the intelligence officer to note changes over time if multiple sketches are made of the same target area. Military sketches provide intelligence sections a detailed, on-the-ground view of an area or object that is otherwise unobtainable. These sketches not only let the viewer see the area in different perspectives but also provide tactically useful details about a target area such as type of fences, road and soil conditions, present depth of streams, and so forth.

Snipers use two basic types of military: the panoramic sketch and the topographic sketch. By definition a military sketch is a reproduction of a target area drawn to scale containing information such as terrain features and manmade structures that are not shown on a map. This being the army there is a standard form, the DA Form 5788-R (Military sketch), that is used to record this information. Students are graded on their sketches and those who cannot produce a usable document are dropped from the course.

A panoramic sketch is a representation of an area or object, drawn to scale as seen from the sniper's perspective. The panoramic sketch is a useful method of recording detailed information about a specific area or a manmade structure. Marginal information is included on panoramic sketches that note important operational and tactical

Range estimation requires a very detailed knowledge of the actual dimensions of objects that later can be used to calculate target distances, and the instructors use the old army "crawl-walk-run" method to teach these skills. Here the students physically measure the horizontal and vertical dimensions of a standard target, known to the students as "Bob."

Now, using the scale built into the M22 binoculars and Leupold spotting scope, each student measures the angular distance of the target and the truck in mils. A simple formula will convert the mil measurement and the known dimensions of the objects to actual range. The process is not quite as accurate as a laser rangefinder, but it doesn't require batteries or special equipment.

details. The marginal data contains enough information to make it understandable and usable, indicating who drew the sketch, what it represents, and other useful details.

As with all drawings, artistic skill is an asset. However, snipers do not need to be landscape artists in order to produce simple but satisfactory sketches. This is a skill that requires constant practice, especially if the sniper is not a natural artist.

A topographic sketch is a representation of an area drawn to scale as seen from above. The topographic sketch gives the sniper a method of describing large areas while showing reliable distances and azimuths between major features. The topographic sketch can also be used as an overlay on the range card. Marginal information contained in a topographic sketch is similar to the data included on the panoramic sketch.

Topographic sketches rely less on artistic skill than do panoramic sketches but demand a knowledge of military maps and the functions of tactical map overlays. Topographic sketches should indicate terrain relief, roads, structures, target reference points, and boundaries.

Observation logbooks are used in conjunction with field sketches and range cards. The observation logbook is a written chronological record of all activities and events that take place in a sniper team's area. This combination not only gives commanders and intelligence personnel information about the appearance of the area but also provides an accurate record of activities in the area.

SNIPER DATA BOOK

A first-shot hit is the goal of the sniper. To achieve that goal, a sniper must understand, above all else, himself and his rifle. Every rifle has distinct performance characteristics, just like every sniper, and the sniper data book is the tool that collects and manages that information. Each data book is a unique record of every shot a specific sniper has fired from a specific rifle, the conditions under which the round was sent downrange and the results of the shot. This data, collected over time, allows the sniper to more accurately predict how he and his rifle will perform under various conditions and to incorporate that knowledge into his shot calculations.

All students are required to have at least one electronic calculator, and many have two, one for backup. The calculators speed up the process of working the range estimation formula. Later, after enough practice, the snipers will easily make the calculations in their heads.

"What do you mean, you can't figure it out?" This instructor, a retired first sergeant, is a civilian contractor who augments the active-duty cadre. Like many of the staff at the school, he's a retired Ranger sniper now working as a civilian instructor and brings a career's worth of experience to training new snipers.

Sniper data books, whether created at the unit level or commercially acquired, are at the basic level a collection of data cards. The data book may also contain ballistics tables, range estimation aids, and other reference material. According to FM 23-10:

> The sniper uses the data cards to record firing results and all elements that had an effect on firing the weapon. This can vary from information about weather conditions to the attitude of the firer on that particular day. The sniper can refer to this information later to understand his weapon, the weather effects, and his shooting ability on a given day. One of the most important items of information he will record is the cold barrel zero of his weapon. A cold barrel zero refers to the first round fired from the weapon at a given range. It is critical that the sniper shoots the first round daily at different ranges.

RANGE CARDS

Range cards are familiar tools to most infantrymen. They are commonly used in defensive positions as an aid to quickly engage targets and to describe the target area.

The range card is a representation of the target as seen from above and includes annotations indicating distances throughout the target area. There are two types of range cards, the preprinted variety with range rings and the field expedient variety that is sketched on any material that is available. The range card gives the sniper a quick reference guide and the means to record information for after-action reports.

KEEP-IN-MEMORY SYSTEM

Snipers must be able to remember details of events they observe, however fleetingly, and report those details accurately. A keep-in-memory system (KIMS) is a memory enhancement exercise in the form of a game. Reportedly Rudyard Kipling invented the game in the

1880s as a method to help messengers remember information. Robert Baden-Powell, the founder of the Scouting movement, described the game in his 1910 book, *Scouting Games.* Canadian army snipers further developed the exercise during World War II.

The conduct of the exercise is described in FM 23-10:

A KIMS game exercise consists of ten variable military items on a table, covered with a blanket, poncho, or anything suitable. Snipers observe the objects when uncovered but cannot touch the items or talk during the exercise.

(1) After a prescribed time, the items are covered, and the snipers write their observations on a score sheet. They write the details that accurately describe the object, omitting unnecessary words. There are many variations that can be incorporated into a KIMS game, such as PT, an extended amount of time between observing and recording,

distractions while observing and recording, or the use of different methods to display items. For example, instead of a blanket use a towel or slides. At the end of the time limit, snipers turn in the score sheets, and trainers identify each item. Snipers describe each object in the following categories:

(a) *Size:* The sniper describes the object by giving the rough dimensions in a known unit of measure or in relation to a known object.

(b) *Shape:* The sniper describes the object by giving the shape such as round, square, or oblong.

(c) *Color:* The sniper records the color of the object.

(d) *Condition:* The sniper describes the object by giving the general or unusual condition of the object such as new, worn, or dented.

(e) *Appears to be:* The sniper describes what the object appears to be such as an AK-47 round or radio handset.

The instructor-to-student ratio is high at the school. Some of the staff observe and coach the students, while others record scores from the many graded exercises.

During week one the new students become accustomed to carrying their rifles and all their gear with them everywhere. They also become accustomed to doing a great deal of mathematics, estimating and measuring targets and ranges, all under the watchful eye of civilian and military instructors.

You can use your sand sock to help stabilize the M22 binoculars, as this student is doing here. The binos have a calibrated scale that may be used to calculate the range to the target, but accurate measurements require a very stable and secure optical device.

After a few days of training and practice, the students take the first of a long series of tests on their ability to calculate engagement distances. Errors within 10 percent of the actual value are considered acceptable.

(2) Snipers receive 1/2 point for indicating that there was an item with some sort of description and the other 1/2 point for either exactly naming the item or giving a sufficiently detailed description using the categories listed previously. The description must satisfy the trainer to the extent that the sniper had never seen the object before. The total possible score is ten points. Experience in the exercise, time restraints, and complexity of the exercise determines a passing score. This is the trainer's judgment based on his own experience in KIMS games.

The first few games should be strictly graded, emphasizing details. When the snipers are familiar with the game pattern, the trainer may make changes. The last game of the training should be identical to the first. In this way, the sniper can see if he improved.

RANGE ESTIMATION
Range estimation is the process of determining the distance between two points. In most situations, one of these points will be the observer's position, while the other may be the target or a prominent feature. In order to accurately calculate a shot on target, the sniper must have some idea of the range to the target. Range estimation is also necessary to complete range cards and military sketches. Laser range finders (LRFs) provide the fastest and most accurate method but sniper teams must not become dependent on this instrument. Teams must be able to estimate range to targets using several different methods and must be able to do it quickly and accurately. The new snipers are taught the following methods:
Map estimation (paper strip)
100-meter unit-of-measure
Appearance-of-objects
Bracketing
Range card
Laser range finder
Mil-relation formula
Combination method

The *map estimation* method is done by placing an edge of a strip of paper adjacent to both points, then penciling in a tick mark at both locations and measuring the distance between them on the map's bar scale. This method requires a map of a suitable scale and knowledge of both locations on the map.

The *100-meter unit-of-measure* method relies upon the sniper's ability to visualize 100 meters on the ground. This method requires constant practice but can be accurate out to 500 meters. For ranges up to 500 meters, the team determines the number of 100-meter increments between the two objects it wishes to measure. Beyond 500 meters, it must select a point halfway to the object and determine the number of 100-meter increments to the halfway point, then double it to find the range to the object.

The *appearance-of-objects* method relies on the sniper's knowledge of an object's characteristic details at different ranges. This method requires constant practice to achieve any measure of accuracy. This method determines range by the size and other characteristic details of the object. For instance, at 200 meters a human body is clear in all details to the naked eye but at 500 meters the body shape tapers and the head becomes indistinct.

The *bracketing* method is used to determine the range of a target that is between two other objects, whose range is known, or if the sniper makes an assumption that the target is no closer than "X" meters and no farther than "Y" meters. The sniper uses the average of those two values as the range of the target. For instance, if the target was between a storage facility 470 meters from the sniper's position and a hill 750 meters from the sniper's position then the estimated range to the target would be 610 meters using this method.

The sniper team can also use a *range card* to quickly determine ranges throughout the target area. Once the target is seen, the team determines where it is located on the range card, and then reads the proper range to the target.

This contractor has a long history with the U.S. Army Sniper School. He was an instructor at the school when he was an active-duty soldier and returned after he retired. He brings decades of practical experience to his instruction, which he delivers in a no-BS fashion. He is widely respected by students and cadre alike.

This is one variation on the prone position taught to sniper school students, a very different position from that taught to millions of earlier soldiers and marines. The body is directly behind the rifle; this helps absorb recoil effectively and keep the weapon on target. Pulling up one knee rotates the chest slightly and makes breathing a bit easier.

Laser range finders (LRFs) provide an extremely accurate and fast method of range estimating a target. However, they require extra equipment and training. Because they are rendered useless by a dead battery, snipers must not rely on this method alone. A common laser range finder for sniper teams is the AN-PVS 6 mini eye-safe laser infrared observation set (MELIOS). The MELIOS weighs 6.5 pounds and is accurate to within 5 meters out to a range of 9,995 meters.

The preferred method of estimating range is the *mil-relation formula*. This method uses the mil-scale reticle located in the M22 binoculars, the GR-12 spotting scope, or in the M3A rifle scope to measure an object of known size. Then using a simple formula the range is estimated. In order to use this method, the team must know the target size, which is converted into a "constant." The constant is a metric measurement so inches are converted to millimeters by multiplying them by 25.4. For example, a 24-inch stop sign would have a "constant" of 610 (24 x 25.4 = 609.6, which is rounded to 610). Once the target constant is known, the team then compares the target size to the mil-scale reticle and uses the following formula:

Constant ÷ Mil Reading of the Target = Target Range (meters).

Using our stop sign example, if the sniper measured the object through his optical scale as 1.5 mils, then the range to the target would be 407 meters (610 ÷ 1.5 equals 406.6666, which is rounded to 407 meters). Snipers collect constants for all manner of objects found on the battlefield and keep those constants in their data books for reference.

The "cheat sheets" in the sniper data book should have multiple measurements for equipment and weaponry. For instance, measurements of combat vehicles should include constants for the height of road wheels as well as the overall vehicle dimensions. A sniper may not have a complete view of a complete weapon system, so he must have constants for component parts of those systems such as the length of main gun tubes on tanks. Constants should also be calculated for the average height of human targets in areas of operation.

Snipers operating in urban environments should calculate constants for the average size of doorways and windows, as well as the average width of streets and lanes in their area of operations.

The *combination* method involves using two or more different methods to estimate range to target. Perfect conditions rarely exist in combat. Therefore, using only one

An alternate prone position keeps the body comfortably behind the rifle, but with legs extended and heels flat on the ground. The students are conducting one of their first live-fire exercises, sighting in from the three hundred-meter line. From now on, such targets will seem extremely easy.

method of range estimation may not be enough. Dead space in terrain limits the accuracy of the 100-meter method. Poor visibility limits the appearance of the object method. By combining two or more methods, a team can arrive at a range estimation that is close to the actual range.

Three factors affect visual range estimation: the nature of the target, the nature of the terrain, and the light conditions when the estimation is made.

A target will appear closer if the object has a regular outline and contrasts with its background. A target will appear more distant if it has an irregular outline, blends with its background, or if it is only partially exposed.

A target will appear closer when it is observed over smooth terrain or if it is observed across a depression, when most of the depression is hidden from view. Objects appear closer when looking uphill or when

Instructors carefully monitor each student for proper position and make immediate corrections of improper cheek weld and firing-hand position.

these suits render the sniper almost invisible even to a trained observer. However, a ghillie suit is, despite its reputation, not a cloak of invisibility and an incorrectly constructed suit looks exactly like what it is, a heap of burlap. A poorly constructed ghillie suit is easily spotted and alerts the enemy that snipers are operating in that area, which often has the unwelcome result of counter-sniper operations.

The first military use of ghillie suits occurred during World War I, when the Lovat Scouts, a Highland regiment of the British army, adopted them for their snipers. The suit has it origins with Scottish gamekeepers who were known as "ghillies." They used the suit as a portable hunting blind.

The ghillie suit gives the sniper a base from which to build on his individual camouflage. The suit breaks up the body's outline and creates a three-dimensional form that allows the sniper to blend in as undetectable as possible into his immediate surroundings. Suits are constructed specifically for the terrain in which they will be worn. A woodland ghillie suit would not work in a desert situation and vice versa.

Students must construct their own ghillie suit while at USASS. Time is allotted at the end of the training day for suit construction, maintenance, and inspection. It is important to remember that the ghillie suit serves as a base for camouflage and is meant to be used with natural vegetation. Vegetation is what allows a sniper to effectively blend into the natural surroundings while minimizing target indicators. The object is not to look like a bush but to look like nothing. The suit does not make the sniper invisible and certainly will not make him bulletproof; it is only a tool to aid the sniper in stalking his target.

INTRODUCTION TO THE M9 PISTOL

Snipers carry the M9 pistol for personal defense. It is a 9mm semiautomatic pistol, designed by Barettta, with a magazine capacity of fifteen rounds. The United States adopted it in 1985 to replace the M1911A1 .45-caliber pistol. During this introductory class at sniper school, students are instructed in the operation and maintenance of the M9 and in practical and advanced shooting techniques.

Pistol marksmanship is a highly perishable skill. When snipers need to use their pistols it usually means that the situation is not good. Training is conducted to simulate the stress of sudden or unexpected situations.

looking down a straight, open road, or along railroad tracks. A target will appear farther if the observer's eye follows the contours of the terrain when observing across a depression, all of which is visible. Objects appear to be farther away when looking downhill or when the field of vision is narrowly confined.

Light can make the target appear closer when a target can be clearly seen, when a target is viewed in full sunlight, or when the sun is behind the viewer. The target will appear farther when it is viewed during limited visibility or when the sun is behind the target.

GHILLIE SUIT CONSTRUCTION

A ghillie suit is a specially made camouflage uniform covered with irregular patterns of garnish or netting that helps the sniper blend in with the surrounding terrain and be hidden from observation. When they are constructed correctly, and augmented with local vegetation,

Sergeant Daniel Porter pays careful attention to advice from one of the instructors during an early live-fire session.

ELEVATION AND WINDAGE HOLD-OFF

In a perfect world, a shooter will adjust the bullet drop compensator (BDC) on his scope for every shot, so that his point of aim would be the point of impact. This is not always possible and there will be many occasions when the sniper will have to apply a technique that is sometimes called "Kentucky windage," when he shifts his point of aim to achieve the desired point of impact. These situations arise when a sniper is confronted with multiple targets at various ranges, when winds are rapidly changing, or when there is limited exposure of targets. Time constraints may force the sniper to employ hold-off techniques during movement or when rapidly reengaging the same target. This technique requires extensive practice to develop reliable accuracy.

Range estimation exercises are conducted on a variety of terrain types. This particular exercise is conducted on the airstrip that is adjacent to the MOUT training facility.

PRACTICAL EXERCISES AND FIELD WORK

During their first week at sniper school, students spend at least twenty hours in practical exercises that reinforce the lessons learned in the classroom. During these exercises, several skills and techniques are incorporated into the same exercise in order to maximize the training value of the time. For instance, a target detection exercise may also incorporate a military sketch exercise and a KIMS game during the same block of instruction. Students spend many hours on their bellies during these exercises as they are conducted under conditions designed to make the new snipers accustomed to observing the world from that perspective.

Each practical exercise is graded in order to assist the cadre in identifying students who are having difficulties and need extra instruction. At the end of the week, a qualification examination is conducted under the same

Intensity and the ability to maintain concentration are common traits among students at sniper school.

Students share experience and knowledge with each other after the conclusion of exercises. The school's Honor Code prohibits students from assisting one another during graded exercises, but afterward there is much discussion among the students.

conditions as the practical examinations. Students who do not pass the qualification exam are given an opportunity to retest. Students must pass every qualification, or retest, at the course in order to graduate. During the first week, the students are tested in target detection and range estimation.

SHOOTING AND RANGE WORK

The first time a sniper takes a newly issued rifle to the range he must adjust and confirm the rifle's "zero." For the M24 this means adjusting the M3A telescope at 100 yards and then confirming the zero by testing it at longer known distances. At sniper school this process is also used to introduce students to the finer points of operating a bolt-action rifle. Although many snipers grew up hunting, there are students in every class who have never operated a bolt-action rifle.

The first shooting exercise that the students engage in is called a spot and shoot drill. The primary purpose of the exercise is not to train the shooter but to train the spotter in how to spot bullet "trace," the visible trail left by the bullet's supersonic wake. The secondary purpose is to train the spotter and shooter to work as a team and develop their dialogue. Each team's dialogue will be slightly different but they all follow a similar pattern. The observer will identify a target and direct the shooter to that target, the shooter will acknowledge target acquisition, the observer will indicate that he is ready to observe the shot, the sniper will indicate when he is ready to shoot, and, finally, the observer will instruct the sniper to shoot with the command "Send it." This process ensures that the sniper is shooting at the same target the observer is watching and that the observer is ready to catch the fleeting glimpse of bullet trace. The spot and shoot exercises allow the team to develop these skills in a structured and measured environment.

SUMMARY OF WEEK ONE

Students who arrive at USASS physically fit and with some unit pretraining tend to fare better during the first week than those students who arrive at the school with little or no idea about the intensity of the experience at Harmony Church. In addition to the classroom instruction, practical exercises, and range work, there is physical training, both formal and informal. At the end of week one, students begin the day with an 8- to 10-mile road march, with full rucksack and a 14-pound sniper rifle, conducted at a pace that only Rangers find comfortable.

It is during that long, fast march that some students reevaluate their desire to carry a long rifle into combat.

The days are long, with the first period of instruction scheduled for 0530 hours, and the cadre try to use every available learning opportunity that is presented during the day, usually created by a student's mistake. Smart students learn from their own mistakes; really smart students learn from the mistakes of others. Most student mistakes are the common "newbie" mistakes and are often addressed with some humor. Mistakes that create a safety hazard such as negligent handling of firearms, however, are not treated lightly and, along with Honor Code violations, may cause a student to be immediately removed from the class and returned to his unit.

The trucks that transport the ammunition are identified by this cautionary placard.

Safety is a major concern at sniper school. If a weapon is found in an unsafe condition, the instructor will remind the class of basic safety precautions while they do a few hundred pushups. Exercise seems to be a remarkable stimulant for memory. *Gregory Mast*

FOUR

Every student is provided with a photograph and reporting form for the area to their immediate front. They have twenty minutes to locate and identify about a dozen objects, each with some military function, and indicate on the form what they have observed and where.

Making the Long Shot:

Ballistics and the Fundamentals of Marksmanship

After students work on their ghillie suits for a week, instructors inspect and evaluate their handiwork. Much of the material for the suits comes from local arts-and-craft stores not normally patronized by warriors.

BALLISTICS

Ballistics, as it relates to sniper marksmanship, is an applied science, a never-ending study of the firing of ammunition, the flight of the projectile, and the effect that projectile has on the target. That statement, however, simplifies an extremely complex and often controversial field of study that, at times, can seem more like a black art than a science. Ballistics is where the predictable (the theoretical trajectory of a projectile) collides with the unpredictable (environmental variables, for instance) when sending a bullet downrange. Most soldiers and marines engage targets at distances too close to really bother about the finer points of ballistics. Long-range, single-shot marksmanship, however, demands a thorough knowledge of ballistics.

This is a complicated topic and what is included in this book is hardly meant to be comprehensive but merely identifies basic concepts and concerns.

Ballistics is classified into three applicable categories for USASS students: internal ballistics, external ballistics, and terminal ballistics. Internal ballistics is everything that happens inside the weapon, from the time the round is loaded into the chamber to the time the bullet leaves the crown of the muzzle. External ballistics is the study of the flight of the projectile from the time it leaves the rifle

Here is a real-world target-detection problem, a photograph made from inside a sniper hide site in Iraq. On the right side of the traffic circle are two white vehicles, one with red fenders. Between them (and not clearly visible in this low-resolution photograph) is an improvised explosive device (IED) team installing a command-detonated device. *Private collection*

until it impacts the target. Terminal ballistics is the study of the projectile's effect on the target, from the time it impacts until the time it ceases movement. A fourth category, forensic ballistics, is not applicable to the course as it is primarily used for medical and police investigations of ballistic evidence.

INTERNAL BALLISTICS

Internal ballistics includes, among other things, the mechanical functioning of the rifle, the interaction of the rifle and the cartridge, the behavior of the rifle and projectile after the cartridge is fired, and the factors that affect cartridge performance. Modern rifle ammunition, or cartridges, consists of seven components, all of which have an effect on internal ballistics. The seven cartridge components are:

Primer: Located in the base of the cartridge, the primer is struck by the firing pin and ignites the propellant powder. This forms a gas-tight seal and prevents hot gases from venting into the rifle chamber. There are two types of primers in military use. The Berdan primer, invented by Hiram Berdan in the 1860s, is a prevalent system for many foreign weapon systems. The United States uses the Boxer primer, invented by Edward Boxer also in the 1860s. Boxer primers allow the spent cartridge case to be more easily reloaded and are usually less corrosive on the rifle barrel than Berdan primers.

An active-duty instructor evaluates a student's ghillie suit. He has added netting to an old BDU shirt, the foundation for additional material, and it must be well secured. The instructors have all been through the class and have built and used the camouflage suits themselves, some in combat.

The construction of the ghillie suit hat gets special attention because it is a crucial factor in successful stalks later in the course. The hat normally will have material that can be draped over the back for good visibility or pulled forward for good camouflage of the face.

Head: The head of the cartridge is solid with a groove that encircles the case. This allows the extractor on the bolt to grip the cartridge and remove the expended case from the chamber of the rifle. Information about the type and manufacturer of the cartridge located on the head is often referred to as a "head stamp." This is important information for the sniper.

Case: Often referred to as "brass," the case houses all components of the cartridge.

Powder: The bullet propellant is generically referred to as powder. Military smokeless powder for small arms ammunition generally comes in two flavors, Single based, which is made by combining nitric acid and cellulose (cotton fibers) to create nitrocellulose, and double based, which combines nitrocellulose and nitroglycerin. The powder is categorized into three basic types, based on the shape of the powder particles, of ball, flake, and extruded. The shape of the powder particle has an influence on how the powder burns and creates the expanding gases that drive the bullet down the barrel.

Shoulder: The shoulder is where the cartridge narrows and provides the function of setting head space in the M24. If the head space is too short, ammunition that is in specification may not chamber correctly. If head space is too large, the cartridge case may rupture, possibly damaging the weapon and possibly injuring the shooter.

Neck: The neck holds the bullet securely to the cartridge case.

Bullet: The bullet is the projectile that is sent downrange. Most military bullets have lead cores surrounded by a copper jacket. Snipers use bullets that have special features that increase their aerodynamic performance, making them more accurate at long range. The M118 special ball (SB) bullet weighs 173 grains and has a full metal jacket and a "boat tail," which is intended to eliminate the drag-inducing vacuum that is created as a bullet travels downrange at supersonic speeds. The M118 long range (LR) bullet weighs 175 grains and has a boat tail and a ballistic hollow point. The ballistic hollow point reduces drag on the bullet as it travels through the

On Monday of week two the students assemble at Maertens Range for their fifth class session on target detection, and the course becomes a bit more challenging. Students search the target area for military hardware that would indicate an enemy's presence. Once the students detect the material, they identify and plot it on a photograph of the target area.

atmosphere but does not cause the bullet to expand inside a target, which would prohibit it from military use.

Each bullet has a ballistic coefficient, which is used to measure bullet efficiency. This number is mathematically derived by considering the bullet's weight, shape, and speed, as well as the material it is made of. A perfect bullet, or the "Standard Bullet," would have a coefficient number of 1. The M118 SB has a coefficient of .446, the M118 LR has a coefficient of .505.

Muzzle velocity is the speed of the bullet as it leaves the muzzle of the weapon and is normally measured in feet per second (fps). The muzzle velocity for M118SB or M118LR when fired through an M24 SWS is approximately 2,600 fps. The five radials in the barrel of the rifle cause the bullet to spin, which stabilizes the projectile during flight. The 1:11.2-inch twist rate causes the bullet to spin at 166,920 rpm, or 2,782 rps. Change in the ammunition's temperature changes the muzzle velocity, so snipers are trained to monitor this variation. For instance, a 20-degree change in ammunition temperature results in a 50 fps change in muzzle velocity, which will affect the bullet's trajectory. Snipers keep velocity charts for a variety of conditions to assist them when they are planning a shot.

When a bullet accelerates down a rifle barrel, the barrel reacts a bit like a bell being rung. This is called barrel harmonics and each barrel has a specific and unique harmonic. The barrel vibration is caused by the bullet being propelled down the radials of the bore and out the muzzle. It causes an undulating motion of the barrel within the stock that is sometimes called "barrel whip." Barrel harmonics influence where the bullet is going to strike, especially when the rifle has not been fired previously (cold bore). This is why the barrels of most sniper rifles are free floating.

EXTERNAL BALLISTICS

External ballistics is where the weird stuff happens. Once a bullet leaves the rifle, numerous factors influence the flight of the projectile and the sniper team must make judgments about these unseen environmental conditions between them and the target. FM 23-10 defines the common terms used when describing external ballistics:.

Line of Sight: A straight line from the eye through the aiming device to the point of aim.

The students begin their observation by methodically inspecting the area first with the unaided eye, getting a wide view of the area and noticing suspicious areas and objects.

The second phase of the search process uses each student's spotting scope to examine the area in closer detail, especially suspicious objects or areas identified in the first phase of observation.

Line of Departure: The line defined by the bore of the rifle or the path the bullet would take without gravity.

Trajectory: The path of the bullet as it travels to the target.

Midrange Trajectory/Maximum Ordinate: The highest point the bullet reaches on its way to the target. This point must be known to engage a target that requires firing underneath an overhead obstacle such as a bridge or a tree. Inattention to midrange trajectory may cause the sniper to hit the obstacle instead of the target.

Bullet Drop: How far the bullet drops from the line of departure to the point of impact.

Time of Flight: The amount of time it takes for the bullet to reach the target from the time the round exits the rifle.

Retained Velocity: The speed of the bullet when it reaches the target. Due to drag, the velocity will be reduced.

A bullet's trajectory is influenced by the following factors:

Gravity: Once the projectile leaves the rifle barrel gravity applies a constant, downward pulling force on the projectile, eventually pulling it to the ground. Because this factor is constant, it can be compensated for fairly accurately through the use of a bullet drop compensator (BDC).

Drag: The aerodynamic resistance a projectile encounters as it moves through the air. The amount of drag varies because temperature, humidity, altitude, and barometric pressure all influence atmospheric density.

Temperature: Temperature affects atmospheric density. Warm air is less dense than cold air. As the

Observing from the prone position makes it very difficult to detect objects on the ground or in the grass, but the students gradually figure out where the ten objects have been hidden, and most are able to identify what they are.

temperature rises, so does the impact point of the projectile.

Barometric Pressure: Like temperature, barometric pressure affects atmospheric density. The higher the barometric pressure, the denser the atmosphere and the greater the drag on the projectile.

Altitude: As altitude increases, the density of the atmosphere decreases. A sniper needs to be aware of his altitude and any significant changes in altitude during operations.

Wind: The atmospheric condition that has the greatest effect on ballistic trajectories. The amount of effect depends on the time of flight, wind direction, and wind velocity. Wind will normally have the most effect on the projectile from the midrange point to the target. The ability to estimate wind speeds is a critical skill for snipers and observers, and they use mathematical formulas to calculate wind velocity into minutes of angle for adjusting their rifle optics.

A minute of angle is defined as a proportional unit of measure equal to one-sixtieth of a degree. One minute of

Rarely are objects hidden in plain sight, but a 40mm training round has been placed inside the glass globe normally covering a light bulb. More difficult to detect is the M249 ammunition drum deep in the shadows of the latrine.

An M249 ammunition drum is located next to the gravestone in this target-detection exercise.

angle (MOA) is equal to approximately 1 inch for every 100 yards of range. The M3A and the ANPVS10 is graduated in 1 MOA increments for elevation and 1/2 MOA increments for windage.

Bullet trace is the visible wake of a supersonic projectile as it flies through the air. Observers use trace to issue corrections to the shooters. It is caused by a high pressure front of compressed air in front of the bullet and turbulence around the sides. It is very similar to and looks much like the wake of a boat. However, it is visible for only as long as it takes the bullet to reach the target and can be seen only with an optical devise with a high degree of magnification. The ability to see bullet trace is important, because if impact is not seen, trace is what the observer will use as a basis for corrections to subsequent rounds.

TERMINAL BALLISTICS

Terminal ballistics is what happens when the bullet slams into its target and it is affected by the velocity of the projectile, the stability of the projectile, and the angle of entry. This is useful for making decisions about shot placement. Other factors include barriers that may need to be penetrated before hitting the target such as glass or protective armor. Terminal ballistics determines whether the target is killed instantly, in the case of a no reflex head shot, or whether the target survives for a short time after being shot.

FUNDAMENTALS OF MARKSMANSHIP

Sniper marksmanship is an extension of basic rifle marksmanship, governed by the same fundamental principles. Accuracy is developed through consistency of actions. The sniper has two basic tasks when shooting. First he must properly orient the weapon toward the target, and then he must fire the weapon without moving it. The four fundamental principles that govern this process are steady position, aiming, breath control, and trigger control. FM 23-10 is an excellent reference and is summarized here.

Steady Position: Consistency is impossible in the absence of a steady firing position. The sniper must be able to relax and concentrate when preparing to fire, something that is not possible if his position is wobbly. There are eight elements to creating a steady firing position; when done correctly, these elements enhance the sniper's ability to achieve a first-round hit.

(1) *Non-firing hand.* Use the non-firing hand to support the butt of the weapon. An effective method is to use a sand sock with the non-firing hand and to place the weapon butt on the sock. This reduces body contact with the weapon. To raise the butt, squeeze the sock; to lower it, loosen the grip on the sock.

(2) *Butt of the stock.* Place the butt of the stock firmly in the pocket of the shoulder. A shooting pad on the shoulder can reduce the effects of pulse beat and breathing, which can be transmitted to the weapon.

(3) *Firing hand.* With the firing hand, grip the small of the stock. Using the middle through little fingers, exert a slight rearward pull to keep the butt of the weapon firmly in the pocket of the shoulder. Place the thumb over the top of the small of the stock. Place the index finger on the trigger, ensuring it does not touch the stock of the weapon. This avoids disturbing the lay of the rifle when the trigger is squeezed.

(4) *Elbows.* Find a comfortable position that provides great support.

(5) *Stock weld.* Place the cheek in the same place on the stock with each shot. A change in stock weld tends to cause poor sight alignment, reducing accuracy. Do not remove the cheek from the stock after firing, if possible.

(6) *Bone support.* Bone support is the foundation of the firing position.

(7) *Muscle relaxation.* When using bone support, the sniper can relax muscles, reducing any movement that tense or trembling muscles could cause. Aside from tension in the trigger finger and firing hand, any use of the muscle generates movement of the rifle and its optics.

(8) *Natural point of aim.* The point at which the rifle naturally rests in relation to the aiming point is called natural point of aim. One method for checking for natural point of aim is for the sniper to close his eyes, take a couple of breaths, and relax as much as possible. Upon opening his eyes, the scope's cross hairs should be positioned at the sniper's preferred aiming point. Because the rifle becomes an extension of the sniper's body, it is necessary to adjust the position of the body until the rifle points naturally at the preferred aiming point on the target.

Aiming: The sniper begins the aiming process by aligning the rifle with the target when assuming a firing position. The three phases of aiming are eye relief, sight alignment, and sight picture.

(1) *Eye relief* is the distance from the sniper's firing eye to the rear sight or the rear of the scope tube. Care must be taken to avoid "scope bite," the embarrassing injury a sniper incurs when he is struck by the scope tube during recoil. The best aid to consistent eye relief is maintaining the same stock weld from shot to shot.

(2) With telescopic sights, *sight alignment* is the relationship between the cross hairs (reticle) and a full field of view as seen by the sniper. The sniper must place his head so that a full field of view fills the tube, with no dark shadows or crescents to cause inaccurate shots. He centers the reticle in a full field of view, ensuring the vertical cross hair is straight up and down so the rifle is not canted.

(3) The *sight picture* is the relationship between the reticle and full field of view and the target as seen by the sniper. The sniper centers the reticle in a full field of view. He then places the reticle center of the largest visible mass of the target. The center of mass of the target is easiest for the sniper to locate, and it surrounds the intended point of impact with a maximum amount of target area.

Target detection exercises are conducted from the prone position. The world looks like a very different place when viewed from 18 inches above ground level.

After working on the problem of detecting targets in a rural environment, the students head off to the McKenna MOUT site, a training area designed for practicing military operations in urban terrain.

When sight alignment and picture are perfect (regardless of sighting system) and all else is done correctly, the shot will hit the center of mass on the target. With an error in sight alignment, however, the bullet is displaced in the direction of the error. Such an error creates an angular displacement between the line of sight and the line of bore. This displacement increases as range increases; the amount of bullet displacement depends on the size of alignment error.

An error in sight picture is an error in the placement of the aiming point. This causes no displacement between the line of sight and the line of bore. The weapon is simply pointed at the wrong spot on the

Once again each student is provided an observation form and photograph of an area to his front, but this time the hidden objects are fiendishly placed deep in the shadows of larger buildings and under vehicles, often with very little exposure.

There are six objects partly visible to the students in the area depicted in this photo—a rifle barrel, ammunition drum, 25mm cartridge case, "clacker" for a M18 Claymore, smoke grenade, and bipod.

target. A sniper's rifle in a supported position moves much less than an unsupported one, but both still move in what is known as a wobble area. The sniper must adjust his firing position so that his wobble area is as small as possible and centered on the target.

Breath Control: While shooting, snipers must learn to control their breathing, which can cause the rifle to move during respiratory cycles. The sniper must time his shot so that it occurs during a natural respiratory pause.

Trigger Control: Trigger control can prove to be the most difficult aspect of sniper marksmanship. The trigger must be pulled with a smooth gradual motion, without disturbing the lay of the weapon or changing either the sight picture or sight alignment.

Applying the fundamentals of marksmanship increases the chances of sending a well-aimed bullet downrange. Once mastered, additional skills can make a first-round target engagement more certain. Chief among these skills are several post-firing actions collectively referred to as "follow-through." From FM 23-10:

a. Follow-through is the act of continuing to apply all the sniper marksmanship fundamentals as the weapon fires as well as immediately after it fires. It consists of—

   (1) Keeping the head in firm contact with the stock (stock weld).

   (2) Keeping the finger on the trigger all the way to the rear.

   (3) Continuing to look through the rear aperture or scope tube.

   (4) Keeping muscles relaxed.

   (5) Avoiding reaction to recoil and/or noise.

   (6) Releasing the trigger only after the recoil has stopped.

b. A good follow-through ensures the weapon is allowed to fire and recoil naturally. The sniper/rifle combination reacts as a single unit to such actions.

Whenever a sniper fires his rifle he "calls the shot" or predicts where the round should impact on the target. Proper follow-through will aid in calling the shot. The dominant factor when calling the shot is the final focus point: the last place on the target where the reticle was located when the weapon discharged.

Snipers apply the fundamentals of marksmanship in a method called the integrated act of firing. The integrated act is a logical approach to firing a single round that helps the sniper develop consistent habits, firing each shot the same way. The integrated act of firing can be divided into four distinct phases: the preparation phase, the before-firing phase, the firing phase, and the after-firing phase. From FM 23-10:

a. Preparation Phase. Before departing the preparation area, the sniper ensures that—

   (1) The team is mentally conditioned and knows what mission they are to accomplish.

See the M16 barrel and fore-end in this view? They are the most easily seen of the objects in this exercise, readily visible in the loophole to the right of the phone booth. More difficult to spot, but easier than many objects, is the body of an M67 hand grenade without the fuse assembly.

The Leupold spotting scopes are essential to closely inspect and identify suspected objects. The students learn to avoid guessing and to record only what they can actually see.

(2) A systematic check is made of equipment for completeness and serviceability, including, but not limited to—

(a) Properly cleaned and lubricated rifles.

(b) Properly mounted and torqued scopes.

(c) Zero-sighted systems and recorded data in the sniper data book.

(d) Study of the weather conditions to determine their possible effects on the team's performance of the mission.

b. Before-Firing Phase. On arrival at the mission site, the team exercises care in selecting positions. The sniper ensures the selected positions support the mission. During this phase, the sniper—

(1) Maintains strict adherence to the fundamentals of position. He ensures that the firing position is as relaxed as possible, making the most of available external support. He also makes sure the support is stable, conforms to the position, and allows a correct, natural point of aim for each designated area or target.

(2) Once in position, removes the scope covers and checks the field(s) of fire, making any needed corrections to ensure clear, unobstructed firing lanes.

(3) Makes dry firing and natural point of aim checks.

(4) Double-checks ammunition for serviceability and completes final magazine loading.

(5) Notifies the observer he is ready to engage targets. The observer must be constantly aware of weather conditions that may affect the accuracy of the shots. He must also stay ahead of the tactical situation.

c. Firing Phase. Upon detection, or if directed to a suitable target, the sniper makes appropriate sight changes, aims, and tells the observer he is ready to fire. The observer then gives the needed windage and observes the target. To fire the rifle, the sniper should remember the key word, *BRAS*. Each letter is explained as follows:

(1) *Breathe.* The sniper inhales and exhales to the natural respiratory pause. He checks for consistent head placement and stock weld. He ensures eye relief is correct (full field of view through the scope; no shadows present). At the same time, he begins aligning the cross hairs or front blade with the target at the desired point of aim.

(2) *Relax.* As the sniper exhales, he relaxes as many muscles as possible, while maintaining control of the weapon and position.

(3) *Aim.* If the sniper has a good, natural point of aim, the rifle points at the desired target during the

Above: A student studies his observation report after having it graded. Many of the students will miss one or two of the ten objects. In some classes, up to 10 percent of the students wash out of the school due to failure on the target-detection exercises.

Mentoring is a constant process. The active-duty and civilian instructors coach each soldier on the process of observation and answer questions. The class is broken down into groups of about a half-dozen students, each with a mentor who helps with problems during the challenging course.

respiratory pause. If the aim is off, the sniper should make a slight adjustment to acquire the desired point of aim. He avoids "muscling" the weapon toward the aiming point.

(4) *Squeeze.* As long as the sight picture is satisfactory, the sniper squeezes the trigger. The pressure applied to the trigger must be straight to the rear without disturbing the lay of the rifle or the desired point of aim.

    d. After-Firing Phase. The sniper must analyze his performance. If the shot impacted at the desired spot (a target hit), it may be assumed the integrated act of firing one round was correctly followed. If, however, the shot was off call, the sniper and observer must check for possible errors, which include the following:

(1) Failure to follow the keyword, BRAS (partial field of view, breath held incorrectly, trigger jerked, rifle muscled into position, and so on).

(2) Target improperly ranged with scope (causing high or low shots).

(3) Incorrectly compensated for wind (causing right or left shots).

(4) Possible weapon/ammunition malfunction (used only as a last resort when no other errors are detected).

MOVING TARGETS

Enemy soldiers rarely respond positively to a polite request that they remain still long enough for the sniper to shoot them. Targets on the battlefield tend to move quickly and erratically, often giving the sniper a partially exposed target for a limited amount of time. Engaging a moving target is a skill that can be developed and maintained only through constant practice.

The first concept that must be learned in order to engage a moving target is "leading." The cross hairs are placed ahead of the moving target because the sniper is shooting where the target will be when the bullet arrives downrange, not where the target is when the round is fired. Four factors need to be considered when leading a target:

Speed of target: The speed of the target will determine how far it will move while the bullet is in flight.

Faster moving targets will require a greater lead than slower moving targets.

Angle of target's movement: A target walking perpendicular to the bullet's flight path will move a greater distance than a target moving at an angle toward or away from the sniper. A target moving at a 45-degree angle to a sniper will have less lateral movement than a target moving at a 90-degree angle. If a target is moving toward or away from the shooter then no lead is necessary but the sniper must remember that the target range is constantly changing.

Range to the target: The farther away a target is from the shooter, the longer the flight time of the bullet. The longer the flight time, the more the lead must be increased. For instance, an M118LR 7.62mm bullet takes 0.7 second to travel 500 meters, during which time a quickly walking target could easily move 4 feet. Estimate range to target at point of engagement, not point of detection.

Wind effects on the trajectory of the round: The direction of the wind must be considered in relation to the direction the target is moving. The lead could be increased or decreased, depending on whether the target is walking into or against the wind.

Snipers can calculate the lead required for a moving target if they know the range to the target and the speed that the target is moving. The target range gives the sniper the time of flight for his bullet and the target's speed allows the sniper to estimate how far the target will move during that time. The formula is

Time of Flight x Target Speed (in feet per second) = The Lead (in feet).

For instance, a target at 500 meters (.788 second flight time) walking at a slow pace (4 feet per second) perpendicular to the sniper would require that the rifle be aimed a bit more than 3 feet in front of the target. For aiming purposes, that lead is converted into mils by first converting the lead in feet to meters, then dividing the lead in meters by the range to the target in meters, giving the sniper the lead in mils. This is done because the scale inside the sniper's scope is graduated in mils.

There are four methods used to engage a moving target:

(1) *Tracking:* Tracking requires the sniper to establish an aiming point ahead of the target's movement and to maintain it as the weapon is fired. This requires the weapon and body position to be moved while following the target and firing. This is not the preferred method of engaging moving targets because the weapon must be moved during the process.

Students spend many hours observing the world through optics as part of their training in the basics of sniping. It is a skill that requires practice to perfect and practice to maintain.

(2) *Ambushing or Trapping:* This is the preferred method of engaging moving targets. The sniper establishes an aiming point ahead of the target and pulls the trigger when the target reaches that point. This method allows the sniper's weapon and body position to remain motionless. With practice, a sniper can determine exact leads and aiming points using the horizontal stadia lines in the mil dots in the M3A. It also has the additional advantage that the sniper selects the place and moment of execution. This method is best used when engaging targets who move at a constant speed on predetermined routes such as sentry patrols.

(3) *Tracking and Hold:* The sniper uses this technique to engage an erratically moving target. While the target is moving, the sniper tracks along, keeping the cross hairs centered on the target to the extent possible, adjusting his position as the target moves. When the target stops, the sniper quickly perfects his hold and fires. This technique requires concentration and discipline to keep from firing before the target comes to a complete halt. This method is most effective on stop and go targets such as an infantry soldier conducting 3- to 5-second rushes.

(4) *Firing a Snap Shot:* A sniper may often attempt to engage a target that presents itself only briefly, then resumes cover. Once he establishes a pattern, he can aim in the vicinity of the target's expected appearance and fire a snap shot at the moment of exposure. For instance, a soldier who periodically pops his head into a window and then returns to his covered position would be a good target for this method.

FIVE

During the second week, students spend more than half their time on field exercises, shooting at the range and on evaluated events. This week sees many students wash out of the course, usually due to failures on evaluated events.

Sniper Training: Week Two

The target detection and observation form is used to record the location of each object, as well as its identification, color, condition, and remarks. Students are graded on not only being able to detect the hidden objects but also their ability to record them accurately.

OVERVIEW

Intensive classroom instruction continues during the second week of sniper school. The topics tend to emphasize advanced field craft, tactical employment, and survival. Marksmanship training emphasizes engaging targets at unknown ranges and moving targets. Practical exercises become more physically demanding, as does the physical training.

Experienced instructors mentor students through target-detection exercises by experienced instructors. This civilian instructor has combat experience that dates back to the Vietnam War, and he is able to offer practical, real-world advice to his students, some of whom are young enough to be his grandsons.

CLASSROOM INSTRUCTION

Students spend a bit less time in class during the second week, about twenty hours instead of thirty. During the second week, students receive instruction in:

Camouflage and concealment

Selection, occupation, and construction of sniper positions

Command and control, use, and employment of snipers

Stalking

Moving targets

Tracking and counter-tracking

Survival, escape, and evasion

CAMOUFLAGE AND CONCEALMENT

Camouflage may be key to a sniper's success but it is also fundamental to his survival. Snipers operate in small teams, often isolated from friendly forces, and being

detected by the enemy has a way of wrecking the team's day. Snipers are drilled with the warning that if the enemy is within range, then they are as well. Unlike training ranges where the bullets go in only a single direction, combat is a two-way range. Marksmanship allows a sniper to hit his target; camouflage prevents him from becoming a target.

Camouflage derives from the French word *camoufle*, which means "to disguise." It is a method of deception in which the sniper disguises or conceals himself through the use of paints, nets, or vegetation in order to blend into the background. The three general methods of camouflage are classified as hiding, blending, and deceiving.

Hiding is used to conceal the body from observation by lying behind an object or thick vegetation. This method may also provide cover from direct fire. Blending is used to match the personal camouflage of the sniper with the surrounding area to a point in which the sniper cannot be seen. Deceiving is used to fool the enemy into making false conclusions about the location of the sniper team.

The sniper team uses natural and artificial camouflage. Natural camouflage is vegetation or other materials that are native to the sniper's area of operations. Natural camouflage may be manmade materials if a sniper is operating in an urban area such as debris or trash used to disguise a sniper's position. Artificial camouflage is materials or substances that are produced for the purpose of coloring or covering something in order to conceal it. Camouflage face paint or burlap attached to a ghillie suit would be an example of artificial camouflage. Generally speaking, artificial camouflage is produced in three patterns: striped, blotched, and combination. Striping is used when the sniper is in heavily wooded areas and when leafy vegetation is scarce. Blotching is used when the sniper's area of operation is thick with leafy vegetation. Combination patterns, like the U.S. woodland pattern, are used when moving through changing terrain and it is normally the best all-around pattern. Combination patterns are usually not perfect for any single terrain but are good for most terrain types.

In addition to a sniper's personal camouflage, he must also camouflage his gear, taking care to ensure that the camouflage does not interfere with the operation or use of the equipment. The sniper team also camouflages its equipment. However, the camouflage must not interfere with or hinder the operation of the equipment. The sniper's rifle and team weapons should be camouflaged to break up their outlines. The "drag bag" for the sniper's rifle should be camouflaged with garnish similar to the ghillie suit. Optics the sniper team uses must also be camouflaged to break up the outline and to reduce the possibility of light reflecting off the lenses. Lenses can be covered with mesh-type webbing or nylon hose material. The sniper's rucksack should also be as well camouflaged as his ghillie suit.

Snipers may be forced to improvise and use field-expedient camouflage materials if other means are not available. Mud, natural vegetation, or charcoal may be used if camouflage face paint is not available, for instance. FM 23-10 suggests that walnut stain may be used but most snipers may find that it is too permanent a stain to be used in anything but the most dire emergency. Oil and grease should not be used because they have strong odors that are easily detected.

Just as a sniper detects enemy positions by searching for target indicators, the sniper must be aware of the target indicators that he presents. In a nutshell, target indicators are anything a sniper does or fails to do that could result in his detection by the enemy. Some of the target indicators a sniper may create during operations are:

Almost invisible in the grass, and with the sun glaring on it from behind, one of the items in the target detection problem has been placed just a few feet in front of the observation line. The students are taught to look for clues, like tracks in the early-morning dew, to help find where objects have been hidden.

Sound: Sounds caused by movement, equipment rattling, or talking are easily detected as being out of the ordinary. Small noises may be dismissed as natural, but talking will not. Sounds are most noticeable during hours of darkness.

Movement: Movement is most noticeable during hours of daylight. The human eye is naturally attracted to movement and quick or jerky movements will be detected easier than slow and deliberate movements.

Improper camouflage: The primary indicators of improper camouflage are shine, outline, and contrast with background. Poorly camouflaged optics may cause shine by light reflecting off glass lenses. A sniper must be aware of the area around him and that a regular outline of personnel or equipment is easily detected. Similarly, camouflage should blend with the background in color and texture. Contrast created by inappropriate camouflage is also easily detected.

Each of the objects in the problem has some sort of military function and is familiar to all the students. This is a circuit-testing device for a M18 Claymore mine. Its green color blends effectively with the grass and makes it a challenge for most of the students to spot.

A cartridge case is a very small object, and this one is only partially visible, but seeing one on the ground could provide the sort of meaningful information that sniper teams are expected to collect.

Disturbance of wildlife: Enemy soldiers may be alerted to a sniper's presence by the behavior of animals in the area of operations. Birds suddenly flying away, the sudden stop of animal noise, or animals being frightened are indicators of an unusual presence. Domestic animals such as dogs or farm livestock may also provide target indicators. Dogs are a particular problem for snipers operating in urban areas.

Odor: Snipers should be aware of the odors produced by their actions such as cooking or smoking and the residual odors produced using chemical products such as insect repellent. Scented soap, deodorants, and aftershave lotions should be avoided prior to operations.

In order to be effective, camouflage must blend with the local terrain. In general, the four types of areas that a sniper will operate within are snow, desert, jungle, and urban. In snowy areas, blending is more effective than texture camouflage. Snipers use white coveralls or a combination or over-white bottoms and brown or green top depending on the amount of snow in the trees. In sandy desert areas with little vegetation, snipers use a blending of tans and browns. They also use the terrain and any available vegetation to their advantage. In jungle areas, textured camouflage, contrasting colors, and natural vegetation are all used to best effect. In urban areas, the sniper should use blended colors of mostly shades of gray. Textured camouflage is not as important in this area.

Cover and *concealment* are often used interchangeably but the words have two different meanings. Cover is anything that protects an individual from enemy weapons fire. Concealment is anything that protects an individual from enemy observation. Snipers use a few rules for concealment:

Avoid unnecessary movement
Use all available concealment
Stay low to observe
Avoid shiny reflections
Avoid skylining, which occurs when a sniper's silhouette is visible against the sky
Alter familiar outlines
Observe noise discipline

SELECTION, OCCUPATION, AND CONSTRUCTION OF SNIPER POSITIONS

Selecting a sniper's firing position, or hide, is a deliberate act that is dictated by the tactical demands of the mission and the opportunities offered by the terrain in the area of operations. Snipers occupy the selected position using stealth and deception, because enemy observation will compromise the mission. Constructing the hide is an art form unto itself that can require the sniper team to carry a small hardware store in their rucksacks. It is important that the sniper remember that the enemy is almost always the home team, with the advantage of local knowledge, when planning this process.

SELECTION AND OCCUPATION

The process begins when the sniper team is alerted to its mission. Upon receiving a mission, the sniper team locates the target area, and then determines the best location for a tentative position by using one or more of the following sources of information: topographic maps, aerial photographs, visual reconnaissance before the mission, and information gained from units operating in the area. The sniper team ensures the position provides an optimum balance between the following considerations:

Maximum fields of fire and observation of target area
Concealment from enemy observation
Covered routes into and out of the position
Location no closer than 300 meters from target area
A natural or manmade obstacle between the position and the target area

A sniper team must remember that a position that appears to be an ideal location may also appear that way to the enemy. For instance, church bell towers are good sniper positions only in Hollywood movies. Avoid choosing locations that are:

On a point or crest of prominent terrain features
Close to isolated objects
At bends or ends of roads, trails, or streams
In populated areas, unless it is required

The sniper team must use its imagination and ingenuity in choosing a good location for the given mission. The team chooses a location that not only allows the team to be effective but also must appear to the enemy to be the least likely place for a team position. For example:

Under logs in a deadfall area
Tunnels bored from one side of a knoll to the other
Swamps
Deep shadows
Inside rubble piles

During the mission planning phase, the sniper team also selects an objective rally point (ORP). From this point, the sniper team conducts a reconnaissance of the selected area to determine the exact location of its final position. The location of the ORP should provide cover

The "spoon" from a smoke pot is hidden in plain sight, its bright color and reflective surface making it easier to detect than many other objects, even though it has been tucked away on the back of a street sign.

and concealment from enemy fire and observation, be located as close to the selected area as possible, and have good routes into and out of the selected area. From the ORP, the team moves forward to a location that allows the team to view the tentative position. One team member remains in this location to cover the other team member who recons the area to locate a final position. Once a suitable location has been found, the covering team member moves to the position.

While conducting the reconnaissance or moving to the position, the team:

Moves slowly and deliberately, using the sniper low crawl
Avoids unnecessary movement of trees, bushes, and grass
Avoids making noise
Stays in the shadows, if there are any
Stops, looks, and listens every few feet
Conducts a detailed search of the target area (when it arrives at the firing position)
Starts construction of the firing position, if required
Organizes equipment so it is easily accessible
Establishes a system of observing, eating, resting, and latrine calls
Establishes an escape and evasion plan.

This spent M18 smoke grenade is easy enough to see from here but more difficult to spot from the observation line 50 meters away, where its singed surface blends well with the bark of this tree.

CONSTRUCTION

A sniper's mission always requires the team to occupy some type of position. These positions can range from a hasty position, which the team may use for a few hours, to a more permanent position, which could be occupied for a few days. The team should strive to build its position at night.

Whether a sniper team is in a position for a few minutes or a few days, the basic considerations in choosing a type of position remain the same. The first consideration is the location of the position, with attention given to the terrain and soil type (which will influence how much time is needed for construction) and the enemy location and capabilities (which will determine what type of position to construct). The second consideration is time, both in the length of time the site will be occupied and the amount of time needed to construct the site. The final considerations are personnel and equipment, as they will determine whether construction is or is not feasible in the available time.

Belly and semi-permanent hide positions can be constructed of stone, brick, wood, or turf. Regardless of material, every effort is made to bulletproof the front of the hide position such as packing body armor around loophole areas. In a semi-permanent hide position, logs should be used as the base of the roof. The sniper team places a dust cover over the base, then a layer of dirt, then a layer of gravel, if available. The team spreads another layer of dirt and then adds camouflage. Due to the use of various materials, the roof is difficult to conceal if not countersunk.

To prevent detection, the sniper team should construct an entrance door sturdy enough to bear a man's weight. The construction of loopholes requires care and practice to ensure they afford adequate fields of fire. Loopholes must be camouflaged by foliage or other material that blends with or is natural to the surroundings. It is vital that the natural appearance of the ground remains unaltered and camouflage blends with the surroundings.

A hasty position is used when the sniper team is in a position for a short time and cannot construct a position due to the location of the enemy, or immediately assumes a position. The sniper team uses what is available for cover and concealment. Although a hasty position may be quickly occupied, it offers little in the way of protection from indirect fire and relies heavily on personal camouflage to avoid detection.

When a sniper team is required to remain in position for a longer time than the hasty position can provide, an expedient position should be constructed. The expedient position lowers the sniper's silhouette as low to the ground as possible, but it still allows him to fire and observe effectively. The expedient position requires a minimal amount of construction and conceals most of the body and equipment. It also, however, affords minimal protection from indirect fire and allows very little freedom of movement.

The belly hide is similar to the expedient position, but it has overhead cover that protects the team from the effects of indirect fires and allows more freedom of movement, at the cost of requiring extra time and materials to construct. This position can be dug out under a tree, rock, or any available object that provides overhead protection and a concealed entrance and exit. A well-constructed belly hide may be occupied for twelve to forty-eight hours, depending on the mission.

The semi-permanent hide is used mostly in defensive situations. This position requires additional equipment and personnel to construct. However, it allows sniper teams to remain in place for extended periods of time or to be relieved in place by other sniper teams. Like the belly hide, this position can be constructed by tunneling through a knoll or under natural objects already in place. The semi-permanent hide is completely concealed and offers excellent cover from indirect fire. This type of hide may be occupied for extended periods of time by different teams.

Although the construction of positions may differ, the routines while in position are the same. The sniper and the observer should have a good firing platform. This gives the sniper a stable platform for the sniper weapon and the observer a platform for optics. When rotating observation duties, the sniper weapon should remain in place, and the optics are handed from one member to another.

Sniper data book, observation logs, range cards, and the radio should be placed between the team where both members have easy access to them. A system of resting, eating, and latrine calls must be arranged between the team members. All latrine calls should be done during darkness, if possible. A hole should be dug to conceal any traces of latrine calls.

Snipers are very effective in woodland, desert, and on urban terrain. They can engage targets at longer distances with precision fire and their optics allow them to discriminate individual targets and gather detailed intelligence. The urban sniper is both a casualty producer and an intimidating psychological weapon.

COMMAND AND CONTROL, USE, AND EMPLOYMENT OF SNIPERS

The army and Marine Corps organize and task manage their snipers in slightly different fashions. However, the basic doctrinal missions that they, and snipers from other branches, are assigned are similar. How well snipers are employed often depends less on the capabilities of the individual sniper teams and more on how well the tactical commander is educated on those capabilities.

Special operations forces commanders typically understand what the sniper brings to the party and, as a

This M249 SAW ammunition drum hung on a branch is unavoidable here but nearly invisible when viewed from other angles, where its form blends with the dark shadows and bark of trees at Coolidge Range.

result, SOF snipers are employed creatively. Conventional infantry commanders, who are often less familiar with the real capabilities of their organic sniper assets, may not employ their shooters in capacities that utilize their full potential. It may be up to the individual sniper or his section leader to educate a senior officer that Tom Berenger movies are not a good template for tactical sniper employment. Good communicators make good ambassadors for the trade and that could make the difference between real missions outside the wire and bogus missions guarding the inside of a forward operating base (FOB).

A properly employed sniper team can disrupt enemy movement; influence enemy decisions or actions; and instill fear, cause confusion, and significantly lower enemy morale. Factors that influence the sniper's employment include the commander's intent, common sense, flexibility, imagination and freedom of action, planning, and execution. Snipers may be assigned missions in offensive operations, defensive operations, and in stability and support operations (SASO).

As well as capabilities, commanders must also be aware of the limitations of sniper teams. There are a limited number of teams available for tasking, which can lead to overtasking if not managed correctly. Teams have limited sustainability, mobility, and defensive firepower if they are isolated by enemy forces. Insertion techniques used will greatly impact what kind of load the team can carry into the mission. Sniper teams are often dispatched into battle carrying excessive loads.

Regardless of whether the sniper's task is defensive or offensive, commanders, sniper employment officers, and sniper team leaders take a number of factors into consideration when planning a mission. Generally, they are:

General nature of combat/mission
Enemy sniper capabilities
Terrain and weather conditions
Distance of friendly to enemy units/depth of influence
Degree of initiative shown by enemy
Number of teams available
Support available to teams
Degree of planning completed
Amount of coordination accomplished

STALKING

Stalking is an art that probably dates back to the earliest human ancestors, when the hunter armed with stone

For many practical field exercises, the students line up on a length of engineer tape stretched between two tent pegs. This ensures that each soldier is the same distance from the items to be described and that none has an unfair advantage.

weapons used stealth to get close to his prey and caution to avoid the other predators in the forest. The popular mythology of the sniper is dominated by the image of a heavily camouflaged sniper noiselessly creeping through a forest, invisible to his prey until his presence is announced with a single, deadly rifle shot. Both the army and Marine Corps teach the traditional methods of woodland and open terrain stalking during their basic sniper courses. These methods were developed from hard-learned lessons of wars past and are still applicable to the current conflicts of the early twenty-first century. Snipers deployed to the urban rabbit warrens of Iraq or the mountains of Afghanistan will need to learn new techniques for stalking the enemy but the basic concepts remain the same.

Stalking, in its broadest definition, describes the movement of a sniper from a position of relative safety, such as an ORP, to a position where he can observe and engage his target, undetected by enemy forces. Although specific techniques may vary, certain maxims will always dictate the sniper's actions. Above all else, the sniper must assume that his area of operations is under enemy observation and behave accordingly. A sniper and his team's movement should be slow and deliberate. Undue haste may compromise a mission and students are constantly reminded that "Slow is fast and fast is dead." Every movement should be planned, punctuated by frequent stops to look and listen. When possible, snipers should move when disturbances or distractions will cover their movement such as gunfire, explosions, aircraft, ground vehicle traffic noise, or anything that would conceal the team's movement from the enemy.

Students at USASS are instructed in a variety of individual movement methods, most involving crawling along the ground as low as possible. Among the various crawls are the sniper low crawl, the medium crawl, the high crawl, and a hands and knees crawl. There are specific walking techniques as well. The only time a sniper should be running is when he is being pursued by the enemy. Students are also trained to use terrain and vegetation to their advantage when moving, by keeping as much cover between them and their target as possible.

Common mistakes during stalking that compromise a sniper's position include:

Overhead Movement: This occurs when a sniper causes vegetation, bushes, or small trees to move as he crawls beneath them. An observer may spot this anomalous movement, especially if there is little or no wind in the area of operations.

Parallel Movement: Movement that is parallel to the target area is much easier to detect than movement directly toward the target.

Turkey Necking: This occurs when a sniper elevates his head above vegetation in order to observe the target, much like a wild turkey looking over an object in the wild.

Tree Cancer: A sniper in a ghillie suit hiding at the base of a tree looks out of place to a trained observer who may be searching for him. The ghillie suit looks like an out of place growth on the tree, hence the term *tree cancer.*

PRACTICAL EXERCISES

During the second week, students begin to combine the various skills that they have been taught through practical exercises. Students encounter their first field craft exercises, starting with concealment exercises in the piney woods of Fort Benning. Their brand-new ghillie suits will make their debut during the second week of training.

The survival practical exercise places students into an unexpected situation with minimally adequate tools to deal with the situation. For instance, in the winter the class may be stripped to PT shorts and boots in the freezing cold and given a single fire starting kit. The class will be allowed to dress only after one randomly chosen student is able to light a fire with the materials provided. The class that I observed conducted this exercise during a balmy January morning where the temperature was an unpleasantly warm 27 degrees Fahrenheit.

RANGE WORK

The second week of training brings the students their first graded test of marksmanship, called Record Fire 1, shooting targets at unknown distances from 300 to 800 meters. This event tests the students' ability to estimate distance and wind, communicate as a team, and engage the targets in a short period of time. The class spends at least two days on the range practicing before the qualification event. As with every other graded event, students who cannot meet the minimum standards are dropped from the course; the marksmanship events generally seem to create a higher level of anxiety among the class.

The event is conducted by placing the student teams along the firing line in numbered lanes. Many targets are visible downrange, scattered over the heavily textured and wooded terrain, at various distances ranging from 300 to 800 meters from the firing line. Ten slender steel silhouette targets are used for qualification.

Each target is engaged after the instructor running the event has identified it. The instructor identifies the target to be engaged and then gives the shooting relay two minutes to arrive at a firing solution. During those two minutes, the student team must find the correct target among the many downrange, estimate the range and wind, and adjust the scope for the firing solution.

At the end of the two minutes, the instructor gives each lane an individual fire command, such as "Lane two, engage." The shooter has ten seconds from that command to shoot at the target. Failure to shoot within that ten seconds counts as a miss. Four instructors are observing the targets and they give the primary instructor the determination of hit or miss. If the shooter misses the target with the first round then he is instructed to reengage and has ten seconds to send a second bullet downrange.

The event is scored 10 points for a first-round hit, 5 points for a second-round hit, and no points for a miss. Students require a minimum of 70 points to qualify.

SUMMARY OF WEEK TWO

The first week of school was spent mostly in the classroom, reviewing the basics and learning new concepts. During the second week, students spend more than half their time on field exercises, shooting at the range and on evaluated events. Students begin to learn the skills of stalking and applied field craft that are the hallmark of a sniper. It is during this week when the first students wash out of the course, usually due to failures on evaluated events.

Everything gets more complex as the course progresses. Marksmanship skills are tested when students are presented with targets at unknown distances. Training exercises are often conducted following a lengthy road march to the training area. These little strolls give students plenty of time to reflect on their desire to be a sniper, the burden of a full rucksack and sniper rifle providing extra motivation for introspection. For many students, the rifle's novelty and "coolness" wears off after the first ten miles.

The cumulative effects of physical fatigue start to manifest themselves during the second week of training. Students who have completed Ranger school tend to fare somewhat better than those who haven't during the early phases of sniper training because they have experience with the effects of fatigue. This advantage usually lasts until the third week of training.

SIX

This is the body of a practice M67 fragmentation grenade, minus the fuse assembly. It is easy enough to identify here but much harder when it is fifty meters away.

Target Detection and Selection

A student in camouflage is preparing for a field exercise.

TARGET DETECTION

As a simple matter of battlefield survival, most sniper targets go to great lengths to avoid detection. Therefore, snipers must be trained in disciplined observation techniques in order to detect and locate the smallest indicators of enemy activity. Target indicators can be material such as the normal debris of military operations (discarded ration packages, expended ammunition, etc.) or camouflaged military hardware, and they can be behavioral such as crowd behavior in an urban environment. Observation is a planned, systematic process in which the sniper views an area for target indicators. Snipers are taught that the four elements of observation are awareness, understanding, recording, and response.

A 20mm training cartridge is easily overlooked when it is tucked into bleachers where its shape, color, and texture are very similar to its surroundings.

A 40mm grenade is a bit harder to miss when it is in the sunlight and its blue projectile contrasts with the aluminum bracket on which it has been placed.

Claymore mines are one of the easier items to discover in the target-identification exercises, especially when they are left entirely in the open, as this one has been.

Awareness is being consciously attuned to a specific fact. A sniper team must always be aware of its surroundings and take nothing for granted. The team also considers certain elements that influence and distort awareness. An object's size or shape could be estimated inaccurately if it is viewed incompletely. Distractions degrade the quality of observation. Active participation or degree of interest can diminish over time due to boredom or fatigue. Physical abilities have limitations such as the amount of time an observer may use optics before inducing eye strain or fatigue. Environmental changes affect accuracy when making estimations of size or distance. Imagination may influence the accuracy of observations, especially over lengthy periods of observation.

Understanding derives from a sniper's life experience, which includes education, training, practice, and experience. It enhances the team's knowledge about what should be observed, broadens the team's ability to view and consider all aspects of the sector it is observing, and aids in the evaluation of information collected during observation.

Recording is documenting and recalling what was observed. Usually, the sniper team has mechanical aids such as writing utensils, sniper data book, sketch kits, tape recorders, and cameras to assist in recording observed events. However, the most accessible method is memory. The sniper's mental ability to record, retain, and recall what he has observed can be a critical skill. There are several factors that affect a sniper team's ability to record what has been observed. Foremost among these factors is the amount of training and practice in observation a sniper has received. Observation skills are gained through experience and are perishable if not practiced. The length of time between observing and recording can seriously affect the accuracy of the report. Finally, a sniper's oral and written communication skills may affect the ability to convey messages accurately.

Response is action or actions that a sniper team takes based on the information gathered during observation. It may be as simple as recording information in the sniper's data book or observation log. Perhaps the information needs to be relayed immediately to the tactical commander. The sniper may decide that the information warrants squeezing a trigger and sending a bullet downrange or that it is time to pack up shop and clear out. This is why judgment and experience are critically important attributes of a sniper. It can mean the difference between success and failure in combat, where the consequences are unforgiving.

As stated earlier, observation is a systematic and detailed method of visually searching an area for target indicators. Snipers employ two types of search methods: hasty searches and detailed searches.

A hasty search is the first phase of observing a target area and is conducted immediately upon occupying a sniper position. A hasty search consists of quick glances of specific points, terrain features, or other areas that could hide the enemy, looking for the most obvious positions first. The sniper then quickly begins searching the area closest to the team's position and working outward toward the target area, with binoculars and the unaided eye. The primary purpose of the hasty search is to detect any obvious indicators of enemy activity that might present a threat to the sniper team. When the observer sees or suspects a target, he uses his spotting scope for a detailed view of the target area. The telescope should not be used to search the area because its narrow field of view would take much longer to cover an area. The telescope's stronger magnification can cause eye fatigue more quickly than binoculars.

The detailed search begins immediately after a hasty search has been completed. A detailed search is a more thorough search of the target area, using 180-degree area or sweeps, 50 meters in depth, and overlapping each previous sweep by at least 10 meters to ensure the entire area has been observed. The search begins in the area closest to the sniper team position.

This cycle of a hasty search followed by a detailed search should be repeated three or four times. This will familiarize the sniper team with the area that it is observing. Each additional search will give a closer look at various points, where an indicator may have been overlooked previously. After the initial searches, the observer should view the area, using a combination of both hasty and detailed searches. While the observer conducts the initial searches of the area, the sniper should record prominent features, reference points, and distances on a range card. The team members should alternate the task of observing the area about every thirty minutes.

The sniper team has at least three optical tools to assist in observation. Binoculars and spotting scopes are the primary tools, but the sniper may also use his rifle scope if necessary. At USASS students are trained using M22 binoculars and the Leupold GR#12 spotting scope.

The M22 binoculars give the sniper a wide field of view with relatively low magnification. This allows the sniper to observe large areas for longer periods of time without noticeable eye fatigue. The features of the M22 are:

50mm objective lens
7 power magnification
Separate eyepiece adjustments

An upper hand guard from an M16 looks a bit like a branch when observed from a distance, but this is another one of the objects that the sniper students will have to find, identify, and accurately describe.

Diopter scales on each eyepiece
Adjustment for inter-pupillary distance
Millradian scale reticle for range estimation
Protective covers for eyepiece lenses
Laser protective filters

The light, compact, and weatherproof Leupold GR#12 12-40x60mm tactical spotting scope is ideally suited for use as part of a sniper team. With powerful and bright optics, the GR#12 has variable magnification from 12 to 40 power and features a Leupold mil dot reticle for both range estimation and tactical cooperation with the shooter. The telescope enables the sniper to define objects at greater distance once they have been detected using the binoculars. The high magnification allows the sniper to peer into shadows and dark areas. The high power and small field of view make it unsuitable for viewing large areas for long periods of time due to instability and eye fatigue.

Observation during twilight and nighttime requires different techniques than during daytime. According to FM 23-10:

> Twilight induces a false sense of security, and the sniper team must be extremely cautious. The enemy is also prone to carelessness and more likely to expose himself at twilight. During twilight, snipers should be alert to observation post (OP) locations for future reference. The M3A telescope reticle is still visible and capable of accurate fire 30 minutes before beginning of morning nautical twilight (BMNT) and 30 minutes after the end of evening nautical twilight (EENT).

Snipers cannot solely rely on night vision devices for observation after sunset. No matter how bright the night may be, the human eye cannot function at night with daylight precision. It takes about half an hour for the eye to adapt to darkness and snipers should be aware of factors that can affect their night vision. Night operations require preparation and a team cannot immediately move from a lighted tactical operations center (TOC) to a darkened firing position. Lack of vitamin A impairs night vision. However, taking vitamin A immediately before a mission will not improve night vision capability because the vitamin takes a great deal of time to be absorbed by the body. Colds, fatigue, narcotics, smoking, and alcohol all diminish a sniper's night vision. Exposure to bright lights during a mission will require the sniper to readapt to the darkness.

A student from the Ranger Regiment intently studies the observation area for hidden targets through his Leupold spotting scope. The spotting scope is one of many specialized items of gear that sniper teams use.

Using the mil-dot pattern in the spotting scope along with the known dimensions of objects he has observed, the student is able to calculate the distance to the object using a simple formula.

Real-world observation in a combat environment applies the lessons taught at sniper school with the added feature of targets that can shoot back.
Harry Martinez, Shadow Team

Off-center vision and scanning are two techniques snipers use to assist observation at night. Off-center vision is the best method for observing at night. It is the technique of focusing attention on an object without looking directly at it. If the eyes are focused on different points around an object, about 5 to 10 degrees away from it, then peripheral vision will provide a true picture of the object. The scanning method involves looking at just one point off the object and scanning around the object in a circular pattern. By scanning around the object, the image is focused on a greater area of the rod region thus making the image more defined.

The sniper team may occasionally use artificial illumination for observation, and shooting, during nighttime operations. Common examples are artillery illumination fire, flares, campfires, or lighted buildings. Illumination rounds may come from artillery or mortars, such as the 81mm M301A2 illuminating cartridge that provides 50,000 candlepower. Trip flares or handheld flares may also provide temporary illumination of the target area. Poorly disciplined enemy soldiers may use campfires, or battlefield damage may create fires. These opportunities give the sniper enough illumination for observation and aiming. In urban areas, the sniper can use lighted buildings to observe and eliminate occupants of the building or personnel in the immediate area of the light source.

TARGET SELECTION

Target selection is, ideally, a deliberate six-step process that evaluates a target's priority and the probability of successfully engaging the target, among other things, and is made after careful observation of the target area. However, the real world is rarely an ideal place and the uncertainty of combat may force the sniper team to make the most of fleeting opportunities. A rapidly moving target may not loiter until a positive identification is confirmed. Any enemy soldiers who pose a threat to the sniper team instantly become high-priority targets. FM 23-10 details the six steps in this process:

Threat to the Sniper Team. The sniper team must consider the danger the target presents. This can be an immediate threat such as an enemy element walking upon its position or a future threat such as enemy snipers or dog tracking teams.

Probability of First-Round Hit. The sniper team must determine the chances of hitting the target with the first shot by considering the following:

Distance to the target.
Direction and velocity of the wind.
Visibility of the target area.
Amount of the target that is exposed.
Amount of time the target is exposed.
Speed and direction of target movement.

Certainty of Target's Identity. The sniper team must be reasonably certain that the target it is considering is the key target.

Target Effect on the Enemy. The sniper team must consider what effect the elimination of the target will have on the enemy's fighting ability. It must determine that the target is the one available target that will cause the greatest harm to the enemy.

Enemy Reaction to Sniper Fire. The sniper team must consider what the enemy will do once the shot has been fired. The team must be prepared for such actions as immediate suppression by indirect fires and enemy sweeps of the area.

Effect on the Overall Mission. The sniper team must consider how the engagement will affect the overall mission. The mission may be one of intelligence gathering for a certain period. Firing will not only alert the enemy to a team's presence, but it may also terminate the mission if the team has to move from its position as a result of the engagement.

The sniper's ability to discern high value, key targets on the battlefield and engage those targets with precision rifle fire is the basis for his reputation of deadly efficiency. As has been demonstrated many times in the past, a single, well-placed shot can be worth a battalion of troops on the line. Key targets can be identified by actions and mannerisms, positions within the formation, rank or insignias, or equipment being worn and carried. Key targets include not only enemy personnel but weapons systems and equipment as well. Key targets are prioritized based on their tactical value and the threat they pose to sniper teams. From FM 23-10:

Snipers. Snipers are the number one target of a sniper team. The enemy sniper not only poses a threat to

Sniper hides in urban environments typically offer very limited fields of view. The risk with such hides is that an enemy may be able to attack the hide without being seen, approaching to close range, and then throwing in a grenade or firing through the loophole. Many snipers report attempted attacks on their positions.

friendly forces, but he is also the natural enemy of the sniper. The fleeting nature of a sniper is reason enough to engage him because he may never be seen again.

Dog Tracking Teams. Dog tracking teams pose a great threat to sniper teams and other special teams that may be working in the area. It is hard to fool a trained dog. When engaging a dog tracking team, the sniper should engage the dog's handler first. This confuses the dog, and other team members may not be able to control it.

Scouts. Scouts are keen observers and provide valuable information about friendly units. This plus their ability to control indirect fires make them dangerous on the battlefield. Scouts must be eliminated.

Officers. Officers are another key target of the sniper team. Losing key officers in some forces is such a major disruption to the operation that forces may not be able to coordinate for hours.

Noncommissioned Officers. Losing NCOs not only affects the operation of a unit but also affects the morale of lower ranking personnel.

Vehicle Commanders and Drivers. Many vehicles are rendered useless without a commander or driver.

Communications Personnel. In some forces, only highly trained personnel know how to operate various types of radios. Eliminating these personnel can be a serious blow to the enemy's communication network.

Weapon Crews. Eliminating weapon crews reduces the amount of fire on friendly troops.

Optics on Vehicles. Personnel who are in closed vehicles are limited to viewing through optics. The sniper can blind a vehicle by damaging these optic systems.

These men are at extremely close range and the scene is quite typical of the view observed by snipers. You can spend hours watching casual and innocent activity, then suddenly be confronted with someone with an IED or other weapon and the need to engage immediately.

Communication and Radar Equipment. The right shot in the right place can completely ruin a tactically valuable radar or communication system. Also, only highly trained personnel may attempt to repair these systems in place. Eliminating these personnel may impair the enemy's ability to perform field repair.

Weapon Systems. Many high-technology weapons, especially computer-guided systems, can be rendered useless by one well-placed round in the guidance controller of the system.

The projectiles used as a component of the M118LR cartridge have a small, open tip. Their apparent similarity to banned hollow-point bullets prohibited by the Geneva Convention led to a brief restriction on their use in combat. The open tip only makes them more accurate and does not affect their expansion. The restriction was quickly lifted.

SEVEN

While the students are firing on the unknown-distance range, one of the instructors puts some rounds through a SR-M110 semi-automatic sniper rifle system (SASS). This one is equipped with the Schmidt-Bender scope, a model similar to that adopted by the Marine Corps.

Sniper Training: Week Three

Master Sergeant Frank Valez, the school's legendary "first-shirt" (first sergeant), demonstrates his version of the prone position. Valez is one of many former members of the 75th Ranger Regiment among the cadre at Army Sniper School.

OVERVIEW

The third week of sniper school usually finds fewer students standing in formation at the start of the training week. Some students will have failed one or more graded events, others will not be able to keep up with the demanding physical pace, and very occasionally there will be students who violate the honor code or safety rules. Even though students are supposed to be thoroughly screened by their command before they arrive at school, the occasional problem child gets through the cordon and will be returned to his unit as a discipline drop.

Less time is spent in the classroom and more time is spent on practical exercises and at the range during the third week. Students have only four formal periods of

Instruction during the third week gets serious, with go/no-go tests in shooting, target detection, range estimation, and other skills in the classroom and out on the ranges. Target-detection tests become more demanding, the targets are better hidden, and the students must complete forms to a higher standard than before.

It's a dirty job, but somebody has to do it. During construction of a new classroom facility, the school didn't have enough restrooms for the students, and several Porta Potties were delivered for temporary use. When it is necessary to do anything around the school by manual labor, the students are the ones who do it.

instruction in the classroom. The majority of their time is spent creeping through the woods in ghillie suits, trying not to be seen by the watchful cadre. Students practice and qualify on moving targets during this training week, as well.

CLASSROOM INSTRUCTION
Students spend about eight hours in formal classroom instruction during week three.

Students receive instruction in:
Alternate firing positions
Counter-sniper operations
Fundamentals of reconnaissance
Foreign weapons

ALTERNATE FIRING POSITIONS
During sniper school, the majority of the students' shooting is done from the prone position with a bipod supporting the rifle. Once the student leaves school and enters the real world, however, he will find that shooting from a comfortable, stable prone position is more often the exception than the rule. On the battlefield, the sniper must assume a steady firing position with maximum use of cover and concealment, using whatever material or support is available. Considering the variables of terrain, vegetation, and tactical situations, the sniper can use many variations of the basic positions.

There are certain defined styles of alternate positions such as the Hawkins or the Seated European, but the

With ghillie suits almost complete, the students march off like shaggy bears to an open field for their first class in covert movement techniques. Each of these garments represents many hours of work and a lot of creative effort. Although few will ever be used in combat, the lessons learned about covert movement and tactical hides will pay off on real-world missions.

sniper is limited only by his imagination when responding to the tactical situation. He may need to rest the rifle on his observer while firing, which requires that the sniper and observer synchronize their breathing so the rifle is not jostled off target.

Students are instructed in more than twenty specific types of alternate positions at school. They may get to use as many as eight during the alternate position range exercise. During stalking exercises, they use whatever individual position is necessary and the stability of that position is evaluated as part of the student's score for the exercise. The real learning, however, occurs at the sniper's unit, during training and in combat. As with most other sniper skills, this is one that requires frequent practice to master.

COUNTER-SNIPER OPERATIONS

Enemy snipers present the same deadly threat to friendly forces that our snipers present to them. Enemy sniper activity can hinder movement, create confusion and continuous personal fear, and disrupt operations and mission preparation. They force the commander to divert a significant number of assets to deal with a small number of enemy forces.

There are four basic steps to counter-sniper operations. First, the commander and snipers must identify the threat. Then they must make an assessment of the enemy sniper to determine what type of sniper they are facing. That will allow the sniper to determine appropriate countermeasures. Finally, the snipers will plan and execute the mission.

The first step is to determine if there is actually an enemy sniper operating within the area of operations. The commander must carefully examine the battlefield intelligence indicators to determine if there is an enemy sniper threat. Some key indicators are:

Enemy soldiers wearing special camouflage clothing.

Enemy soldiers with weapons in cases or drag bags.

Enemy soldiers who have weapons with long barrels, scopes, or bolt actions.

Relatively effective single shots fired at key personnel.

79

Above: The human face is normally readily recognized at a great distance. Its oval shape, the reflection of sun from skin, and the distinctive profile and skin color all help an observer identify a potential target at great range. Camouflage face paint is one tool for reducing these recognition factors. These student snipers have selected colors that match the local terrain and have applied them in ways that help break up normal visual patterns.

A lack of or a marked reduction in enemy activity during the time of well-aimed single shots.

Personnel have noticed reflections of light or shine (from optics) with no enemy presence (usually from non-obvious positions).

Intelligence, patrol reports, or reports from other sources of small groups of enemy (usually one to three men) operating within the AO.

Discovery of single expended cartridge casings of the proper caliber. Casings will often have different markings from that nation's standard issue ammunition.

Discovery of hasty or prepared hide positions.

Once it has been determined there is an enemy sniper threat, the next step is to determine the type of enemy sniper present. When determining the type of enemy sniper, the range of attacks, effectiveness of fire, and the location of enemy sniper positions should be taken into consideration. Snipers from the opposing team are categorized into three types.

The Well-Trained Sniper: An enemy who has been specially selected, trained, and equipped with a modern scope-mounted sniper rifle. These individuals are expert shots and are trained to engage selected targets with precision rifle fire. They are capable of hitting targets at a distance of 1,000 meters and are skilled in avoiding detection. These individuals are rare in an irregular insurgent force, but do exist.

The well-trained sniper may be employed alone, as a team, or as part of a hunter/killer element. This sniper often moves into an area and trains other men to serve as shooters. This is the most dangerous adversary to counter, and requires an extensive amount of planning, coordination, and support to eliminate.

The Trained Marksman: A trained soldier who is an above average shot. He has some knowledge of field craft, and is usually armed with a standard issue weapon or scoped version of the standard issue weapon. He is often found operating in urban environments and is similar to the U.S. Army's Squad Designated Marksman. He may be employed individually or in teams to create confusion, cause casualties, or harass and disrupt the flow of operations.

On the gun, Staff Sgt. Harry Martinez is a former marine, now a U.S. Army National Guardsman, and a police sniper in civilian life. He made about thirty kills during a one-year deployment while assigned to one of the most successful sniper sections in the history of the U.S. Army, Shadow Team of 3rd Battalion, 69th Infantry, 3rd Infantry Division, and later to the 101st Airborne (Airmobile). *Harry Martinez, Shadow Team*

The sniper low crawl is the most covert of movement techniques, and also the slowest. It is used when close to the enemy, when there is little cover or concealment, and when moving into a final firing position. The body is kept as close to the ground as possible, with legs together and the weapon held by its sling. The sniper moves forward by pulling himself forward with his fingers and pushing with his toes and the sides of his feet.

The sniper high crawl is faster than the low crawl but less covert. The sniper's body is supported by his elbows and knees, with the torso off the ground and the rifle cradled in the sniper's arms. The high crawl is used when the terrain provides limited concealment but there is enough vegetation to screen the sniper in this position.

The Armed Irregular: The armed irregular has little to no formal military training and no formal training in long-range marksmanship. He is usually a member of an irregular or paramilitary force and may or may not carry his weapon openly. He may go to great lengths to avoid detection as a sniper or combatant. His fires are normally not accurate, and he seldom deliberately targets specific individuals. The armed irregular is intimately familiar with his area of operations and uses it to his advantage.

After the enemy sniper threat has been identified and classified, the proper countermeasures must be emplaced. Countermeasures are classified into two types. Passive countermeasures include all actions the unit takes to reduce the likelihood of casualties inflicted by the enemy sniper. Active countermeasures are those actions taken that directly relate to the elimination of the enemy sniper threat.

Passive countermeasures are largely the common-sense practices of a tactically competent unit. Some common measures include:

Avoid setting routines or patterns

Hold meetings during hours of limited visibility or under cover and concealment

Avoid having soldiers in large groups in the open or standing in line

Hang blankets/covers over windows to protect individuals inside from observation

Place supplies under cover and concealment

Do not salute or wear rank and insignia

The hands-and-knees crawl is faster and is used when more vegetation and concealment are present. The sniper carries his rifle in one hand, the scope in his armpit, and supports himself on his knees and one hand.

Maintain a large number of observation posts (OPs)

Ensure OPs are properly equipped with adequate optics for day and night operations

Clear and occupy buildings around static positions to eliminate potential sniper positions

Maintain active patrols

The first rule of engagement when facing an enemy sniper is to use the maximum amount of force available in accordance with the rules of engagement (ROE) and collateral damage considerations. The sniper on sniper "duel" makes a great movie but should be considered the

Ghillie suits are only one part of a sniper's camouflage and need to be "dressed" before making a stalk. Navy SEAL snipers call the process "vegging up." The sniper adds and removes, as necessary, fresh leaves and grass from the immediate area of his route, and a careful sniper will often replace materials as he moves from an area of one type of vegetation to another.

An active-duty instructor carefully scans the training area for any signs of student snipers—any movement, unnatural colors or contrast, noise, or outlines. When he sees something suspicious, he will use his radio to direct one of the other instructors, called "walkers," to the spot. If his suspicions are correct, the student fails the stalk and is sent back to the start line.

last tactical option, especially when facing a well-trained sniper. The most effective counter-sniper operations will combine all assets available to the commander. Operational security in ongoing operations preclude a detailed discussion of the techniques used when eliminating a sniper threat.

Counter-sniper operations follow the same planning process as all military operations. The sniper team leader should interact closely with the operations and intelligence officers when planning these missions due to his knowledge of sniper operations. The planning process has five steps:

Study the possible sniper threat
Determine enemy sniper patterns
Develop a course of action
Conduct coordination
Execute the mission

FUNDAMENTALS OF RECONNAISSANCE

The secondary mission of snipers is the collection and reporting of battlefield information. Reconnaissance patrols and missions are a basic tool for accomplishing this task. Reconnaissance patrols provide timely and accurate information on the enemy and terrain. They confirm the leader's plan before it is executed. Units on reconnaissance operations collect specific information (priority intelligence requirements [PIRs]) or general information (information requirements [IRs]) based on the instructions from their higher commander.

What's wrong with this picture? Well, the student's hands are un-camou-flaged, and their bright tone and color will be an easy target-identifier for the instructors, carefully watching four hundred meters up the hill. The ghillie suit has almost no garnish, and, although it matches the dead grass well, the sniper should have garnished it with fresh green leaves that match the area where he has set up his final firing position.

Somewhere in the middle of this photograph is a student sniper on his first graded stalk. The terrain is the easiest of all the ground the students will cover, with heavy cover and lots of concealment in shallow depressions of the terrain. As a demonstration of the effectiveness of movement techniques, instructors wearing bright clown outfits have made successful stalks and shots on this range.

Students who have problems with any of the graded shooting events
will get an opportunity to fire again and hopefully make a passing
score. Because the spotter's role in sniper engagements and training is
so important, the school knows that sometimes a spotter will make
incorrect calls and adjustments that result in the shooter's misses.

Recon patrols are generally broken down into two
elements, the reconnaissance team and the security team.
Reconnaissance teams reconnoiter the objective area
once the security team(s) are in position. Normally these
are two-man teams (buddy teams) to reduce the possibility of detection. Security teams provide security for
the reconnaissance teams while they are operating near
the objective. The security teams must be in position
prior to the recon teams nearing the objective. Recon and
security (R&S) teams are normally used in a zone reconnaissance, but may be useful in any situation when it is
impractical to separate the responsibilities for reconnaissance and security. When a sniper team conducts a
reconnaissance patrol, it operates as a single R&S team.

The stalking exercises require students to fire two blank cartridges from
their final firing positions. The blanks produce a small visual signature—
a flash and a bit of smoke—that can betray the sniper's position if the
observer is looking in the right direction.

By the third week, all the students have put hundreds of rounds through their M24s and are comfortable in the sniper's version of the prone position, very close to the ground.

The three general types of recon patrols are area, zone, and route.

An *area* reconnaissance is conducted to obtain information about a specific location and the area around it. The location may be given as a grid coordinate or an objective on an overlay. In an area reconnaissance, the recon element uses multiple vantage points around the objective from which to observe it and the surrounding area. The recon element can pinpoint the objective, establish a limit of advance, obtain detailed information about the objective, or operate as a surveillance team. After the recon element has gathered all of the required information, reached their limit of advance, made enemy contact, or the allocated time to conduct the recon has elapsed, all elements return to the ORP. All elements report their observations to the platoon leader or the recorder. Once all information is collected, it is disseminated to every soldier and reported to higher HQ.

A *zone* reconnaissance is conducted to obtain information on the enemy, terrain, and routes within a specified zone. Zone reconnaissance techniques include the use of moving elements, stationary teams, or a series of area reconnaissance actions.

Moving Elements: The platoon plans the use of squads or teams moving along multiple routes to cover the entire zone. Methods for planning the movement of multiple elements through a zone include the fan, converging routes, and successive sectors.

Stationary Teams: Using this technique, the sniper employment officer (SEO) advises surveillance teams on possible locations where they can collectively observe the entire zone for long-term, continuous information gathering.

Multiple Area Reconnaissance: The SEO tasks each of his elements to conduct a series of area reconnaissance actions along a specified route.

"Spotter up!" is the call informing the shooter that he can send his round downrange. Spotters are the key to effective sniper engagements, and the most experienced man on a team will generally be behind the glass instead of the gun.

Although the spotter can't normally see the actual bullet in flight, he can see the momentary disturbance of the air as it passes, a phenomenon called "trace." He can also see the impact of the bullet on some targets—a puff of dust from a hit on the ground or a masonry wall, and a pink cloud of blood and tissue with hits on human targets.

Land navigation is one of the essential skills for anybody in the ground-combat business, and problems in land nav courses are a major cause for student failures in advanced training. Although real-world snipers rely on battery-powered GPS receivers, the traditional lensatic, liquid-filled version never needs batteries and is extremely accurate.

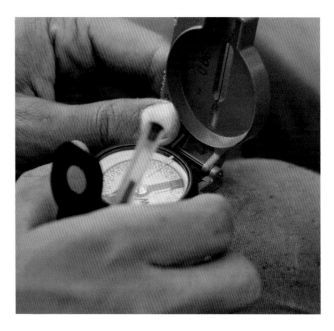

A *route* reconnaissance is conducted to obtain detailed information about a route and all the adjacent terrain or to locate sites for employing obstacles. A route reconnaissance is oriented on a road, an axis of advance such as an infiltration lane, or a general direction of attack. A route reconnaissance results in detailed information about trafficability, enemy activity, NBC contamination, and aspects of adjacent terrain from both the enemy and friendly viewpoints. If all or part of the proposed route is a road, the platoon must treat the road as a danger area. The R&S teams move parallel to the road using a covered and concealed route. When required, teams move close to the road to reconnoiter key areas. The patrol report should be submitted in an overlay format.

Before a patrol leaves, the team leader or SEO determines what information the patrol is required to gather. This is in the form of a PIR. The mission is then tailored to meet that request. All members of the patrol are thoroughly briefed on the commander's intent and information requirements prior to the execution of the mission.

During the patrol, all members continuously gain and exchange all information required. The patrol conducts the reconnaissance without alerting the enemy to his presence. Should the patrol become compromised then the sniper must move, change the plan, or abort the mission. Methods of avoiding detection are:

Minimize movement in the objective area

Avoid paralleling the objective

Move no closer to the enemy than necessary

If possible use long-range surveillance devices or night observation devices

Use cover, concealment, camouflage, stealth, noise, and light discipline

Minimize radio traffic

Immediately after the patrol returns, personnel from higher headquarters conduct a thorough debrief. This may include all members of the patrol and any attached personnel. Normally the debriefing is oral. Sometimes a written report is required.

FOREIGN WEAPONS

Most members of the armed forces have an innate curiosity and interest in weapons, especially those used by foreign forces. The sniper, in particular, must take that curiosity and develop it into an in-depth professional knowledge. He must be familiar with the weapon's country of origin, operating system, functional capabilities, and who uses it. This information allows the sniper to make conclusions based on his battlefield observations. The sniper is also able to use weapons to estimate range, because he knows the length of the weapon. Although the student receives a block of formal instruction on foreign weapon systems, this is merely a brief introduction. The sniper must continually improve this knowledge throughout the length of his military service.

PRACTICAL EXERCISES: STALKING

Stalking exercises pit the individual students against the instructional staff in a high-stakes game. Students who win the game get to stay at school; students who lose are sent back to their units. Briefly, these are timed events in which the student must infiltrate the target area undetected, place a shot on target undetected, and exfiltrate back to the objective rally point before time expires. Students receive a score based on a successful stalk and satisfactory demonstration of skills. Detection during movement is an immediate failure. Students must successfully complete a minimum number of stalks in order to remain in school.

On the 800-meter firing line, half the students are making their record shots while the other half do the spotting chores. Eight hundred meters is generally considered the maximum "effective" range for 7.62mm rifles but snipers will normally be able to consistently make hits on human-sized targets to 1,000 meters and, with .338 Lapua and .300 Win Mag weapons, to 1,400 meters and beyond.

In a typical exercise, students are taken to an unfamiliar training area and dropped off at the objective rally point. There they are briefed on the mission and the rules of the game. This is an individual effort event. Students are prohibited from talking with one another unless it is an emergency such as an injury. During the stalk, the observers may issue the command "Freeze." Students respond to the freeze by immediately stopping and remain in whatever position they were in when the command was issued. If they were standing upright, in the open, then they must remain upright and exposed. Students are prohibited from "melting" during the freeze, which is when they very slowly move to a position of concealment in an attempt to avoid detection. Violations of the rules are treated as a violation of the Honor Code.

During the mission brief, students are issued a map of the target area, two rounds of blank ammunition, and given target assignments. Two instructors are assigned as observers and are seated in the back of a two-ton truck in the target area, watching the area through binoculars. They are also the students' targets. One observer is the "driver," the other is the "passenger," depending on which side of the truck each is seated. Half the students are given the driver as a target, the other half get the passenger as a target. The map contains information about the target area and other instructions such as an emergency azimuth should a student become lost or injured during the exercise. The target area may be as close as 800 meters or as far away as 2 kilometers. Their mission is to "kill" their target and return to the ORP before the time limit expires. At the end of the brief, the students are given ten minutes to prepare before the mission clock starts, which could be anything from two to six hours.

Once the exercise begins, the two observers watch the target area for signs of approaching students. The instructors are expert observers and very little escapes their notice. Wandering throughout the target area are "walkers," who are in radio communication with the observers. When a student is spotted, the observers direct the walkers to the student's location. The walkers provide confirmation of the instructor's observations. If the observer is correct, then the student is told what mistakes he made and is sent back to the ORP. If the observer is incorrect, then the exercise continues, with much good humored radio banter suggesting that the observer visit the optometrist.

The students stealthily navigate to the target area from the ORP. If they manage to make it into the area without attracting the attention of the observers, then they construct their firing position. A firing position must offer concealment yet still have a ballistic and optical loophole. A ballistic loophole means that once the rifle is fired the bullet will have an unimpeded path to the target. An optical loophole means that the sniper can see what he is shooting at clearly. If the student fires a blank round and is not spotted by his target, he will attract the attention of a walker by shouting the identity of his target. For instance, if his target was the driver then he will shout "Driver."

The walker will walk to a point within 10 feet of the student and notify the observer of his location. The observer will examine the area and direct the walker to the shooter if he is detected by the observer. If the student cannot be detected by the observer, then the walker will examine his firing position for stability and check his ballistic loophole. Then the observer will display a placard with an alphabetic letter. The student must be able to correctly identify the letter, which confirms the optical loophole. If he cannot identify the letter, he may be allowed to continue the stalk. If he correctly identifies the letter, then he returns to the ORP, with equal stealth. If he is detected during his return movement, then he will fail the exercise.

This is a difficult exercise but not an impossible one. Occasionally an instructor will make that point by successfully completing a stalk dressed as a circus clown, just to prove that it can be done. Stalking is a life or death skill and how well it is done may determine who lives and who dies. A well-executed stalk means that the target dies. A botched stalk means the sniper dies. In combat, it pays to be a winner.

RANGE WORK, WEEK THREE

Week three is all about moving targets. In combat, targets have the funny habit of refusing to remain stationary. Students at USASS spend their third week on the range learning how to engage moving targets at ranges from 300 to 600 meters. Once they leave school and develop advanced skills, they will be able to engage moving targets to a range of 800 meters. At the end of week three, they have their second marksmanship qualification, Record Fire 2, on moving targets.

SUMMARY OF WEEK THREE

Week three at Harmony Church is the make or break week for marginal students. Most students have established their unique personalities under the close scrutiny of the instructional cadre and the weak performers are well known to both staff and students. Those students who need extra coaching and instruction are given both but the simple fact remains that not every student has the character or skills necessary to become a sniper. Although the U.S. Army has a constant demand for trained snipers, especially during wartime, the cadre at Harmony Church maintain very high training standards, even at the risk of pissing off the chain of command with high attrition rates.

During this week students are introduced to moving targets, because targets on the battlefield have a frustrating habit of not remaining motionless while the sniper works up a firing solution. Students are also critically evaluated on their ability to stalk a target and shoot it without being detected, with most learning the hard way that a ghillie suit is not a cloak of invisibility. Passing these two events provides a real milestone for the students and the collective stress level noticeably lowers afterward.

EIGHT

In the real world of combat sniper operations, ghillie suits are seldom used, and existing cover and concealment are used where and how they are available. Here a U.S. Marine from 1st Battalion, 8th Marines, looks for insurgents running through the streets of Fallujah during Operation Al Fajr, in support of Operation Iraqi Freedom. He and others like him dominated the battle and killed insurgents by the dozens and hundreds. *Lance Cpl. J. A. Chaverri*

On the Run:
Survival, Tracking, and Counter-Tracking

"Vegging up" is an essential part of the preparation for covert movement in wooded terrain. The leaves and grass break up the outline of the ghillie suit and match the sniper's surroundings. Students are taught to change the material as needed during a stalk and to be careful about letting material wilt, because it will sag and take on an unnatural appearance.

There is a distinct likelihood that an individual sniper or his team may become separated from friendly forces during combat missions. Depending on the mission, a sniper may well find himself alone in enemy territory and the subject of an enthusiastic manhunt. His ability to evade capture, survive captivity, or come back home alive will depend on his training, will to live, and a bit of luck.

SURVIVAL, ESCAPE, AND EVASION
Sniper teams often operate in isolation, sometimes deep in Indian Country, reliant upon a quick reaction force (QRF) for defense that most likely will not be "quick" when it reacts. When sniper teams are compromised, they usually do not have sufficient

Above: Fully prepared, a student moves out on a stalk. The two observers who are looking for him are five hundred meters away, up a hill. He can safely walk or run the first hundred meters, and then he'll use terrain to hide him as he moves carefully forward. The last hundred meters or so will often be on hands and knees to a final firing position. Then he will assemble a support for his rifle and make his shots, hopefully undetected.

firepower to engage in a gunfight. The rules of engagement (ROE) may not permit the use of indirect fire such as mortars or artillery, and close air support (CAS) may not be available. At that point, the sniper team must rely on its primary defensive weapon, the ability to run like hell and evade capture or worse. Snipers on the run may be cut off from the support of friendly forces and could well find themselves in situations where their survival depends on their ability to live by their wits. This is why survival, evasion, resistance, and escape (SERE) training is a must for snipers.

SERE training dates to the end of the Korean War, when the air force started a program for aircrews. During the Vietnam War, the program was expanded to include members of the army, navy, and Marine Corps who faced a higher risk of capture than average. This included aviators, special forces, and reconnaissance and intelligence personnel. The program trains students to survive following separation from friendly forces, resist interrogation following capture, escape from captivity, and evade pursuing enemy forces.

Snipers, by virtue of their field craft skills, are generally better prepared than the average soldier or marine for survival situations. *Survival*, in this context, means the continuation of life and existence in the presence of difficult conditions. The ability to survive begins with training and preparation. First, every sniper should have a survival kit with him at all times when on a mission. The kit should be tailored for the area of operations. A typical survival kit includes:

Water packet or means to procure water
Food items and a way to procure food
Fire starting kit
Waterproof matches
Pocket knife
Shelter items
Compass
Signaling device
First-aid kit
Candle

Moving targets are added to the course of instruction during week three, and they are a challenge in two ways. "Movers" are very hard to hit at any range, and especially so at five hundred meters, where a shooter has to calculate his "hold-off" distance accurately or miss the target. Moving targets are also tough for the men who actually move them, because it is extremely hot, uncomfortable work behind the berm.

Students spend many hours learning the basic skills of a sniper while at sniper school. Their real education, however, often starts when they are deployed to combat and must improvise and adapt.

The key factors that influence an individual's survival are primarily psychological and not physical. Assuming that a sniper is not grievously wounded, his body will endure what his mind allows. The brutal truth of the matter is that if the sniper does not have the will to survive then he will die. The psychological and physiological factors of survival are:

Pain: Pain is likely to be a constant companion in a survival situation. Understand its source, recognize it, and concentrate on tasks at hand. Take pride in your ability to operate in the face of pain, make a joke of it if you can.

Cold: Cold numbs the mind as well as the body. Make an effort to get warm and stay warm. Seek whatever shelter may be available, no matter how disgusting it may seem. Build a fire if feasible. Understand how the body loses heat through convection, conduction, evaporation, and radiation.

Heat: Keep head covered in direct sunlight. If the sniper is not acclimated to the heat, it will take at least two to six days to become acclimatized enough to survive. If possible, rest during the hottest hours of the day and travel at night.

Thirst: Thirst is a symptom of dehydration. Almost any stage of dehydration can be reversed by drinking water. It is better to conserve sweat than water, so limit unnecessary activity in situations where water is scarce.

Hunger: Being hungry will affect your morale, attitude, and will to survive. In many areas of the world, you can find edible items that you may not consider food. You may need to overcome cultural prejudices and dislikes against certain foods.

Fatigue: Fatigue reduces mental ability, as any graduate of Ranger school can attest. Rest whenever possible during a survival situation. Conserve energy and get as much sleep as possible.

Boredom: Repetitiveness and uniformity are two sources of boredom. Keep your mind occupied with your survival plan.

Loneliness: Being isolated often leads to a feeling of hopelessness. Self-sufficiency plays a major role in overcoming these feelings.

Students at USASS are given the acronym SURVIVAL to remind them of the rules for living to go on another mission, should they find themselves trapped in hostile territory:

S—Size up the situation: Find a covered and concealed position to concentrate on surviving; security always has priority. Consider your physical state and take care of any injuries. Conduct an inventory of your equipment and size up your surroundings as you begin to make a plan.

U—Undue haste makes waste: Acting merely for the sake of acting, or acting too quickly, may cause your capture or death. Remember that patience is more than a virtue; it may be your ticket home.

R—Remember where you are: During mission planning and the execution of the mission, you should always try to determine the location of the enemy and the areas

04.07.2006 09:12

Staff Sergeant Harry Martinez, leader of Shadow Four sniper team, spots for one of his men from their rooftop hide in Ramadi, Iraq. Although techniques for covert movement and hide construction in the Iraqi and Afghanistani theaters are different than traditional methods, the principles remain valid. Martinez killed three insurgents on an IED emplacement team on his first mission. *Harry Martinez, Shadow Team*

Staff Sergeant James Gilliland is about to send a round downrange with his tricked-out M16 rifle. Gilliland's team accounted for nearly three hundred enemy kills during a six-month period, and he made the longest confirmed kill with a 7.62mm NATO-chambered rifle, 1,250 meters. *Harry Martinez, Shadow Team*

Right: Real-world combat-zone sniper hides are sometimes very different from the school versions. Here an observer in a heavily fortified position scans for enemy activity. Beneath the tripod supporting the scope is an aerial view of the area. Marked on the photo are terrain reference points (TRPs) used to quickly communicate the location of threats and suspicious activity. *Harry Martinez, Shadow Team*

that they control. You should know the location of friendly troops because that will assist in your evasion plan. You should also keep track of the location of water sources. Remember to use your map and compass and always be proactive in the navigation of your team.

V—Vanquish fear and panic: Fear and panic are the greatest enemies in a survival situation. Fear and panic not only take a toll on your mental state but the stress of prolonged fear takes a physical toll. The best way to eliminate fear and panic is through training.

I—Improvise: Improvisation is critical in a survival situation. Improvising is using the wrong tool to do the right job. Get in touch with your inner MacGyver.

V—Value living: Simply put, this is the will to live, the willingness to endure hardship and pain because you want to keep living. Without the will to live you will probably die.

A—Act like the natives: The natives are your best teachers in a survival situation. Understanding local customs is very important. You may need to overcome cultural prejudices, particularly regarding food sources. Also, observing the local wildlife will give clues to survival such as water sources.

L—Live by your wits, but learn the basic skills: Do not confuse adventure training and nice-to-know skills with survival training. The harsh reality is, if you cannot procure water, find shelter and food, start a fire, and accomplish the tasks needed to survive, you will die. A sniper who understands the basic skills will live to fight another day.

Escape and evasion are the next order of business, once initial survival has been addressed. Escape is to get free from; keep away from; or avoid capture, detention, or confinement. Evasion is avoiding capture by trickery or cleverness in hostile or unfriendly areas. Escape and evasion planning should be standard components of mission planning for the sniper. At a minimum, the E&E plan should answer four basic questions: When does the team begin to evade? How will the team evade? Where will the team evade to? How will it get to the evasion extraction point?

There are two categories of evasion. The first, and preferred, category is an assisted evasion. This means that the sniper will get an extraction or receive supplies or assistance from an E&E net. The second, worst-case scenario is the unassisted evasion. This means the sniper is on his own, probably without communication, and it is unlikely that higher headquarters knows the sniper's situation and location.

The five basic types of evasion are:

Evasion by infiltration: The most common method of evasion in which a sniper moves from enemy territory to friendly territory, usually by stealth. Stealth is often necessary to avoid detection by the enemy and to minimize the possibility of having friendly fire come his direction.

Evasion by deep penetration: This method of evasion is when a sniper moves deeper into enemy territory to a recovery point, rather than heading toward friendly lines. This method is very dangerous and requires a great deal of coordination.

Evasion by deception: In this method, the evading sniper may dress as a civilian or use forged documents to cross borders.

Short-range evasion: This takes place within the tactical battlefield.

Long-range evasion: This takes place behind enemy lines or in enemy-controlled territory.

TRACKING AND COUNTER-TRACKING

In addition to his role as a battlefield hunter, the sniper must also be able to act in the capacity of a scout. Tracking the enemy, and in turn, being able to evade the tracking teams of the enemy are basic skills for the modern sniper. Some snipers already have this skill, developed from the experiences of hunting and rural life. Others must learn the fundamentals quickly and develop the skill through constant training. Tracking requires not only intelligence on the part of the sniper, but intuition

Sergeant Harry Martinez from the 28th Infantry, Pennsylvania National Guard, but "chopped" to the 3rd Infantry Division's legendary Shadow Team, scans for targets from Observation Post (OP) Hotel near Ramadi's shooting gallery, the highway through town called MSR Michigan. *Harry Martinez, Shadow Team*

Sergeant Brian Pruett scans for targets in Ramadi. Instead of doing the sniper low crawl and hiding in the weeds, real-world snipers are conducting many urban operations where covert movement involves sneaking through backyards and climbing up the sides of buildings and where hides are set up in homes and abandoned factories. *Harry Martinez, Shadow Team*

Despite all the urban sniper missions, there are places where a ghillie suit would be really useful, and here is a prime example. Both of these guys would virtually disappear if they had their suits, but they are probably back in a locker at the forward operating base. A U.S. Marine and his spotter, both assigned to Reconnaissance Detachment, Command Element, 24th Marine Expeditionary Unit (MEU), Special Operations Capable (SOC), man a 7.62mm M40 sniper rifle from a position covering a vehicle checkpoint in Iraq, during Operation Iraqi Freedom.

and cunning to be able to anticipate the actions of those he is following and those who might be following him.

Tracking is the art of being able to follow a person or animal by the signs that he leaves during his movement. Whether the sniper is the hunter or the hunted, he should ask several questions to determine what techniques he should employ:

How many people am I up against?

How well are they trained?

What is the condition of their health?

What is their morale?

What types of equipment do they have?

When tracking, the sniper looks for indicators his quarry may leave behind. The indicators the sniper discovers can be defined by one of six tracking concepts: displacement, stains, weather, litter, camouflage, and immediate-use intelligence.

Displacement occurs when something is moved from its original position. An example would be a person carrying a heavy load who stops to rest will usually crush grass and twigs. Other signs may be foliage, moss, vines, sticks, or rocks that are broken or moved from natural positions when birds and animals have been flushed from an area. This is also a form of displacement. Footprints are the most common displacement indicators that a sniper will use.

A *stain* occurs when a foreign substance from one organism or article is smeared or deposited on something else. Blood from a profusely wounded soldier

would be the best example of staining. A tracker who is familiar with the characteristics of wounds would be able to determine something about the health of his quarry by the location and appearance of the blood spoor. For instance, if the blood seems to be dripping steadily, it probably came from a wound on the trunk, whereas if the blood appears to be slung toward the front, rear, or sides, the wound is probably in the extremity. A sucking chest wound leaves pink, bubbly, and frothy bloodstains, but the bloodstains from a head wound are usually heavy, wet, and slimy. There are far less gruesome and more mundane examples of this indicator, such as muddy footgear being dragged over grass or urine stains on foliage.

Weather can be the tracker's friend or enemy, depending on how it affects the indicators. Weather may help the sniper determine the relative age of footprints, for instance, or weather can completely obliterate the evidence of that footprint. The tracker should know how weather affects soil, vegetation, and other indicators in his area of operation.

Litter can tell the sniper volumes about the soldier or unit he is tracking. The presence and amount of litter is a good indicator of individual or unit discipline; the type of litter says something about how they are equipped and the condition of the litter can tell the tracker how long it has been there. Litter is anything not natural to the area such as cigarette butts and candy wrappers, or it might be other evidence of human occupation such as the remnants of a campfire or human feces.

Camouflage is evidence that the followed party is employing counter-tracking techniques to baffle or slow the sniper. Some of these methods would include walking backward to leave confusing prints, brushing out trails, and moving over rocky ground or through streams. This would tell the tracker that his quarry may suspect that he is being followed.

The sniper combines all indicators and interprets what he has seen to form a composite picture for on-the-spot intelligence. For example, indicators may show contact is imminent and requires extreme stealth. The tracker can form assumptions based on the indicators that he has found but should never report those assumptions as fact.

Dog tracking teams are the sniper's sworn enemy as they pose a great risk to the sniper's survival if they are present in the area of operation. How the sniper deals with that threat is a matter of some controversy, with no universally agreed-upon answer to the question. Does the sniper shoot the dog, the dog handler, or neither to avoid compromising his position? The right answer seems to be whatever works in the situation. There are some techniques that sniper teams can employ to counter the effectiveness of dog handling teams. Some of them include:

Stay as far from the target area as the situation will allow.

Try to approach the target area from the downwind direction.

Try to travel on hard-packed dry ground or use streambeds when available.

Never leave human waste exposed. Bury waste.

Don't smoke or light fires.

Pack out all trash. Do not leave litter or other materials that would leave a scent.

A band of motor oil around the position may discourage or throw off dogs. Garlic can also be used.

Don't use soap or deodorant before a mission.

Snipers who are being tracked can use three basic counter-tracking techniques. In general terms they are evasion, camouflage, and deception techniques. Evasion involves immediate action drills mostly designed to counter the threat such as rapidly changing directions. Camouflage techniques involve disguising the appearance of indicators the sniper may leave behind. Deception techniques are those tricks a sniper uses to change the appearance of his indicators such as walking backward to intentionally leave footprints.

Sergeant Michael Sistunk and Lance Cpl. Matthew Bateman, part of the reconnaissance marines from the 26th Marine Expeditionary Unit (MEU), Special Operations Capable (SOC), practice stalking techniques with an M40 sniper rifle during Exercise Slunj 2000. The bilateral exercise is designed to build interoperability and cooperation between the U.S. and Croatian military forces. *USMC photo*

Staff Sergeant Harry Martinez, leader of Shadow Four team. Real-world sniper elements are typically composed of ten to twelve men in three or four teams, each team led by an experienced sergeant.

NINE

Week four features the fun and excitement of alternate firing positions and stress-fire. Snipers use alternate firing positions when they need to make a shot in a hurry and there isn't time for arranging conventional support for the weapon. The spotter here uses his rifle scope instead of his spotting scope to observe the target, while his partner uses his back for support.

Sniper Training: Week Four and Week Five

A sniper's eye view of beautiful, scenic, uptown Ramadi. This is typical of many areas of urban Iraq, with many abandoned cars, trash, and clutter—excellent places for hiding bombs or preparing ambushes. *Harry Martinez, Shadow Team*

During the last two weeks of basic sniper training at Harmony Church, students spend the overwhelming majority of their time in the field, putting into practice the theoretical lessons of the classroom.

OVERVIEW: WEEK FOUR

The physical stress of long days and difficult training begins to take its toll by the start of the fourth week at Harmony Church. The road marches to and from ranges, the morning physical training sessions, and the occasional motivational thrashings have usually thinned the herd by this point in the training schedule. Classroom instruction is minimal with almost all the students' time spent on the range or in practical

Staff Sergeant James Gilliland with his section's M107 Barrett. He is in a position on the roof of a headquarters, normally a poor place for a sniper hide because of the position's visibility. Such locations are frequently the targets of enemy rocket-propelled grenade (RPG) and mortar attacks. Snipers don't always get to select their observation and firing positions. *Harry Martinez, Shadow Team*

exercises. The highlights of week four are night marksmanship training on moving targets and urban operations practical exercises.

CLASSROOM INSTRUCTION: WEEK FOUR
Students spend about six hours in three periods of formal instruction in week four. Students receive instruction in:

    AN/PVS-10
    Angle fire
    Urban operations

AN/PVS-10
The AN/PVS-10 night vision sniper scope is an integrated day/night sight manufactured by the Northrop Grumman Corporation. It was developed specifically for the U.S. Army in the early 1990s and entered service by the middle of the decade. It has a fixed magnification of 8.5 power and weighs a hefty 4.5 pounds. Powered by two

This battle-scarred building is OP Hotel, long a well-known sniper hide used by both marines and army personnel. The local insurgents knew of its function long ago and have often attacked it with RPGs, automatic weapons, and even a suicide truck bomber who accidentally blew up the building across the street. *Harry Martinez, Shadow Team*

Week four includes many graded events and failure on any of them will risk a student's place in the class. One of the events is shooting at targets on the unknown-distance course of fire on Coolidge Range. Several instructors monitor each student's performance by carefully watching his targets for hits.

Each scorer calls "Hit!" or "Miss!" for each shot, and they don't always agree. The impacts are sometimes hard to see at five hundred meters and beyond, but a puff of dirt below the steel target will get you a thumbs-down and no credit for the shot.

AA-sized batteries, it has an effective range of 800 meters during daylight operations and 600 meters during night operations. The illuminated reticle is identical to the reticle in the standard Leupold M3A scope, which minimizes training issues.

ANGLE FIRE

Angle firing is the term used to describe techniques used to compensate for the difficulties created when shooting upward or downward at extreme angles such as from a mountainside or tall building. Many snipers are deployed in mountainous and urban environments. These types of operations require engagements at varying elevations and angles. Unless the sniper accounts for the angle and elevation of his position to the target, his round will not hit within one minute of angle (MOA) of its intended point of impact. At ranges of less than 300 meters, the sniper may still hit his target without compensating for this effect but target engagements at greater distances will almost certainly not be successful without taking the angle of engagement into account.

Ordinarily, a sniper zeros his rifle on a level range. When zeroing, the sniper adjusts his scope so the line of sight intersects the bullet trajectory. When the sniper fires at an angle, his line of sight is still located in a perpendicular direction away from the line of departure.

Because of the firing angle, the bullet trajectory no longer intersects the line of sight at the range. In fact the bullet will pass well above the line of sight.

When a sniper is confronted with this situation, he must measure the angle at which he is firing during the range estimation process. There are several tools available for this task, including a clinometer or a "slope doper," and the sniper can also make a field expedient measuring device from his map protractor. Once the angle is determined, the sniper checks a table to find the angle's cosine, which will be used during the calculation of the firing solution. The best, and easiest, method is to use a commercially available device called an angle cosine indicator. This device attaches to the sniper rifle and acts like a circular lever, giving the sniper both the angle and cosine.

Cosine is a trigonometric function that can be used to define a slope. The cosine of an angle can be used to determine the slope's run. In the case of a sniper's firing solution, the actual range to the target is multiplied by the cosine of the angle in order to get the compensated flat ground distance, which will be used to adjust the rifle's optics. For instance, a target is 366 meters from the sniper and the angle of fire is 35 degrees. From his reference table, the sniper determines that the cosine is 0.82. He multiplies 366 meters by 0.82 and arrives at a compensated distance of 300 meters, which is the slope

101

The 9mm hardball cartridge is notorious for its poor stopping ability, but it is better than nothing when you need to control a prisoner or deal with a threat and you can't get to your long gun. Focus on the front sight, put the sight on the target's center of mass, press the trigger, and repeat as necessary till he goes down. Just be careful not to shoot the photographer.

Until recently, the M9 Beretta pistol was pretty much just a fashion accessory worn by officers. Now, with many units participating in urban-combat operations, a large proportion of warfighters carry pistols and often use them in close-quarters combat.

he applies to his optics. This same formula applies whether the angle is uphill from the shooter or downhill.

Angular distortion also creates problems with range estimation. The same method is used to adjust a range estimate derived from the mil relationship formula, because the angle of viewing distorts the perceived size of the constant. Snipers also need to take into account the effects of altitude when calculating the firing solution, as bullets have a higher point of impact as the altitude increases.

URBAN OPERATIONS

As far back as the late 1970s, military thinkers predicted that the most likely conflicts involving ground forces would involve operations in densely populated areas. The nature of the tactical environment in urban areas presents special challenges, limitations, and opportunities to the operating forces. The sniper, while offering many advantages to the tactical commander, must adjust traditional techniques to the limitations of urban terrain. For instance, within an urban environment ranges of observation and fields of fire are reduced and targets are generally exposed briefly at ranges of 100 to 500 meters.

Snipers are extremely effective in urban terrain. Their long-range precision fire can engage targets at a distance and their advanced optics can discriminate individual point targets to save innocent bystanders or protect property. Their observation skills can offer superior intelligence collection capabilities. The sniper is both a casualty producer and an intimidating psychological weapon. Commanders must exercise caution when deploying sniper teams in urban combat because urban areas often become easily isolated by an enemy. Commanders may be restricted in the weapons and tactics that they are allowed to employ to support isolated units.

Buildings are the chief components of urban terrain. They provide cover and concealment, limit fields of fire and observation, and impair movement. It is important to remember that the amount of protection that a building will provide depends on the type of material used in its construction. Underground systems found in some urban areas are easily overlooked but can be important to the outcome of operations. These systems include subways, sewers, cellars, and utility systems.

Civilians will be present in urban operations, often in great numbers. Concern for the safety of non-combatants may restrict fire and limit the maneuver options available to the commander. When the sniper evaluates urban terrain, he should consider the following factors:

Observation and fields of fire
Cover and concealment
Obstacles
Key control points
Avenues of approach
Distribution of building types
Environmental considerations

A variation on the shoulder-support position that provides a little less exposure requires the spotter to lean back on his elbows.

The classic kneeling position, taught to many generations of American soldiers and marines, is still one option for a sniper in combat. It is fairly stable, better than unsupported standing, but far less desirable than firing from the prone position with the rifle supported at the fore end.

Rangers lead the way, and Staff Sgt. Timothy Johns shows the way Rangers from the 75th Regiment get it done—from the front, faster than everybody else. Johns deployed to Iraq soon after completing the class.

A sniper should be given general areas (buildings or a group of buildings) in which to position himself. The sniper himself, however, should be allowed to select the best positions from which to engage. Sniper positions should cover obstacles, roofs, gaps in the final protective fire (FPF), and dead space. The sniper also selects numerous secondary and supplementary positions to cover his area of responsibility.

As part of a larger force, the sniper moves by stealth on secondary streets using cover and concealment of back alleys and buildings. These moves enable him to assist in seizing key terrain features and isolating enemy positions, thus aiding the follow-on unit's entry into the area. Sniper teams may also infiltrate into the city after the initial force has seized a foothold. When infiltrating a target area, snipers should:

- Avoid obvious sniper positions
- Make maximum use of available cover and concealment
- Carefully select a new firing position before leaving an old one
- Avoid setting a pattern
- Never subject the sniper position to traffic of other personnel

Wind estimation in urban areas is challenging because winds are confusing, contradictory, and especially difficult to see. Wind will vary direction and speed, gusting at one level, then blowing steadily at another. Winds become steadier with elevation; gusting may prevail at ground level, but rooftop winds tend to be steady. Downtown streets are actually manmade canyons. Low- and medium-level winds blow down the long axis, parallel to the street. Contradictory winds create considerable confusion at street intersections. Avoid shooting through a major urban intersection on a windy day. If possible, hang small strips of engineer tape or cloth all over the area of operations. Watch how smoke rises from chimneys. Mirage in an urban area can be optically observed on a flat roof even on the coldest days.

PRACTICAL EXERCISES, URBAN OPERATIONS

Fort Benning has several existing, sophisticated MOUT (military operations in urban terrain) training facilities. Most, however, were constructed during the Cold War and resemble a typical central European city. Some improvisation is necessary to simulate the conditions that most of the students are likely to encounter shortly after graduation, when many are expecting deployment to Iraq or elsewhere in the Middle East. Most of the

Here's an alternative firing position that isn't taught at sniper school. Members of this team from the Special Operations Target Interdiction Course (SOTIC) have modified their rifle to attach to a photographer's tripod. SOTIC trains Green Beret, SEAL, and Ranger snipers at Fort Bragg, North Carolina.

instructors are veterans of Iraq, Afghanistan, and Somalia and they incorporate the lessons they learned in combat into the program of instruction. For reasons of operational security in ongoing conflicts, details about these exercises are intentionally vague.

RANGE WORK

During the fourth week students are taught to shoot using alternate firing positions in urban situations, learn basic combat pistol techniques, practice elevation and windage hold-offs, and engage moving targets at night using the AN/PVS-10 scope.

Operations in urban areas dictate that snipers must be capable of delivering accurate fire from whatever stable position is offered by terrain. In this case, the terrain is rooftops and other features of buildings, sewers, rubble piles, and so on. The sniper learns to use the urban topography for cover and concealment, just like he did in wooded terrain such as using the crease in

Stress-firing in the real world is a common problem. This sniper team is from the special operations community, and they are well equipped with highly specialized weapons. They are the rock stars of the armed forces.

When possible, real-world snipers get the best support for the rifle they can find. Sometimes, that is a homemade tripod made specifically for the purpose, and sometimes it is a lightweight photographer's tripod painted and adapted for making a different sort of shot.

This special operations sniper's rifle is chambered for a .300 Winchester Magnum and is equipped with two optical sights. One is a conventional Leupold scope, the other is an EOTech close-quarter combat sight intended for rapid target acquisition at close range or long.

the valley of a roof for concealment as he delivers a shot from a backward leaning position.

Students at USASS are given a brief introduction into basic combat pistol techniques during urban operations. Snipers may find that in Iraq they have to clear rooms of hostiles with a pistol because the only other weapon they have is their long gun. Instructors make it clear that this is a skill that requires constant practice to achieve a level of competence that will keep the sniper alive in a pistol gunfight.

Engaging moving targets at night is similar to daylight, with the same techniques applied to different equipment. The AN/PVS-10 has its own operating characteristics and students use it to qualify on Record Fire 4 from a distance of 200 and 300 meters. If students are lucky, the sky will be clear and the moon full. If they are not that fortunate, then the cadre will provide assistance by illuminating the targets with chem-lights or by setting small fires in the target pits.

SUMMARY OF WEEK FOUR
Week four at USASS is spent largely on preparing students for the situations they will probably encounter shortly after they graduate. Lessons from current and recent combat are incorporated into the training schedule, with recently returned veterans leading the instruction. Many of the students are now veterans as well and the class discussions are deeply informative as experiences and lessons learned are shared. Warfare is constantly evolving and, as stated earlier, success and survival are often the same thing for a sniper.

OVERVIEW: WEEK FIVE
Week five at Harmony Church is relatively light and most students, after a grueling month spent there, are grateful for the small favor. Students will qualify with the M107 long-range sniper rifle, participate in a sniper culmination and final shot event, and graduate.

CLASSROOM INSTRUCTION: WEEK FIVE
Only two classes remain on the training schedule. Five hours well be spent on:

M107 long-range sniper rifle (LRSR)
Sniper sustainment training

M107 LRSR
Commonly known as the "Barrett," after the company that designed and manufactured it, the M107 long-range sniper rifle is an icon of modern sniping.

Although .50 caliber sniper rifles have been in the U.S. inventory for less than twenty years, and the M107 was adopted in 2001, they have achieved a legendary status in the popular imagination. The photogenic menace of the Barrett has made it a favorite of Hollywood filmmakers. Although its reputation for long range accuracy may be slightly exaggerated, the M107 is a devastating weapon system.

By the book, the M107 is a semi-automatic, air-cooled, box magazine-fed rifle chambered for .50 caliber BMG ammunition. This rifle operates by means of the short recoil principle rather than gas. The M107 is useful for traditional anti-personnel roles as well as long range anti-materiel roles and utilizes multiple types of .50 caliber ammunition. At nearly 34 pounds fully loaded, the M107 is considered man-portable by everyone except the guy who has to carry it. It is a direct line-of-sight system capable of providing precision fire on targets at distances up to 1,800 meters. The basic M107 rifle is equipped with bipod, muzzle, break, carrying handle, and 10-round removable magazines. The M107 uses a Leupold 4.5- to 14-power variable scope.

The technical specifications for the M107 are:

- Weight (gun and scope): 28.5 pounds (12.9 kilograms unloaded)
- Overall length assembled: 57 inches (88.9 centimeters)
- Length in takedown mode: 38 inches (86.36 centimeters)
- Barrel length: 29 inches (73.66 centimeters)
- Stock: integral with lower receiver
- Safety: manual thumb-lever
- Muzzle velocity: approx. 2,800 f.p.s.
- Maximum range: approx. 6,800 meters
- Maximum effective range: 1,800 meters
- Muzzle energy: 11,500 foot pounds
- Magazine weight: 3.82 pounds

SNIPER SUSTAINMENT TRAINING
Upon graduation from school, the new sniper has been trained in the basic skills he needs to practice his craft. By no means has he received training in every skill that he will need to survive and thrive in combat. The student's real education begins after he graduates and will need to include topics such as the operation of communications equipment, call for fire procedures, field medicine, intelligence collection, and a host of other topics. The skills that he was taught at Harmony Church are perishable and, at a minimum, will require periodic refresher training.

Although these alternate versions of the prone firing position are not textbook perfect, they work well for the individual shooters.

Recon and surveillance
Log books and debriefing
Standard operating procedures
Survival

At a minimum, the following marksmanship skills should be included in sustainment training:
Known distance
Unknown distance
Moving targets
Cold barrel unknown distance
Elevation and windage hold-off
Alternate positions

RANGE WORK

The student's final marksmanship qualification, Record Fire 4, is with the M107. The student is assigned ten targets at unknown ranges, the closet is 400 meters and the farthest is 1,900 meters. The event is similar in structure to Record Fire 1. Students are given one day to

At a minimum, the following field craft skills should be included in sustainment training:
Stalking
Target detection
Range estimation
Land navigation
Communications

Carting your buddy's wounded carcass out of an ambush area is a reasonably common sniper activity out in the real world, so it is one of the things required of students during the program.

Students run back from the five hundred-meter line toward the six hundred-meter firing points during the stress-fire and alternate-firing-position period of instruction.

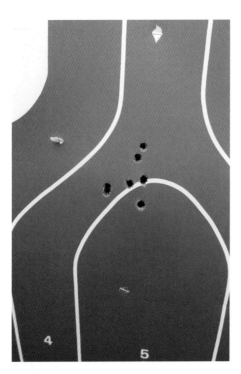

This shot grouping is typical for a student at sniper school, from five hundred meters.

It's back to the pits at Maertens Range for record fire on "movers." Generations of soldiers have fired on this range, and generations of soldiers have had to work the targets behind the butts. Many have left their graffiti on the concrete, some dating back to the 1950s.

gather target information that will be used during the qualification.

SNIPER CULMINATION EVENT AND FINAL SHOT
This is an all-day practical examination that tests the students in every skill they have learned in the previous four weeks. Each class has a different scenario and the scenarios are kept confidential among the instructional staff until the morning of the exercise. Students are often surprised by the requirements of the mission, which requires them to think on their feet and improvise quickly.

GRADUATION
Graduation is a justifiably proud moment for the students who made it through the gauntlet. The class that I observed, Zero Two Zero Seven, started with thirty-five students and graduated twenty-three. Two awards are given to the top students. The Honor Student is the student who graduates with the highest academic average, which combines all the scores of every graded event in written examinations, field craft, and marksmanship. The Top Gun award goes to the student with the highest marksmanship awards. If there is a tie among several students, then the staff will organize a shooting contest and the winner gets the Top Gun prize.

SUMMARY OF WEEK FIVE
Five weeks may seem like a long time to the students at USASS but it is barely enough time to teach the basics of sniping. Graduates of the school carry an ASI of B4 but in reality that means that they are now qualified to learn to become a sniper. The last week of school is short, with both students and instructors fatigued from doing too much in too little time. After graduation, the new Bravo Fours scatter to the winds and return to their units. The school cadre takes a long weekend and gets ready to do it all over again, with a brand new class the following week. They call it "feeding the machine."

An instructor is observing a student team on the known-distance range.

Specialist Theodore Amell of Bravo Company, 1st Battalion, 5th Infantry Regiment, scans the horizon for insurgent activity during a patrol near Mosul, Iraq, on March 31, 2005. *Department of Defense, Tech. Sgt. Mike Buytas, U.S. Air Force*

Opposite page: As the sun sets over beautiful downtown Ramadi, snipers monitor activity along Route Michigan, one of the main supply routes in the area. The M107 Barrett .50-caliber rifle is ready to deal with any local insurgents who decide to behave badly by spraying the area with AK fire or planting an IED down by the traffic circle, a very common event. Dozens of kills have been made from this location, and the M107 has been especially useful against vehicles.

U.S. Army Specialist Chantha Bun, foreground, and Sgt. Anthony Davis, Bravo Company snipers, 1st Battalion, 24th Infantry Regiment, scan for enemy activity at 4 West, an Iraqi police station in Mosul, November 17, 2004. Soldiers from the 1/24 and the Iraqi National Guard secured the police station after attacks by insurgents. *U.S. Army, Sgt. Jeremiah Johnson*

U.S. Army soldiers of 1st Battalion, 24th Infantry Regiment, scan for enemy activity from the top of a building during a combat operation in Mosul, November 9, 2004. The 1/24 is on the offensive searching for and engaging insurgents. While on this offensive, the battalion received indirect fire, small arms fire, and rocket-propelled grenades. *U.S. Army, Sgt. Jeremiah Johnson*

Sergeant Brian Pruett looks for targets from a Ramadi rooftop. Heat is a major risk factor during sniper operations, and avoiding heat stroke requires techniques not taught at school. *Harry Martinez, Shadow Team*

A SOTIC sniper team demonstrates an alternate firing position, using a photographic tripod for support.

Staff Sergeant Harry Martinez uses a wall for cover and concealment while scanning for targets in Ramadi. Members of a sniper team cover assigned sectors and trade off with others on the team to prevent eye fatigue. *Harry Martinez, Shadow Team*

Here is what an observer often observes—a group of people on the street going about what might be routine, innocent activity and what might suddenly turn into insurgent behavior. The range to these people is only about one hundred meters, and the photograph has been taken through mosquito netting, a common material used to prevent enemy observation. *Harry Martinez, Shadow Team*

A typical firing position in Iraq will simply be a loophole in a masonry wall broken out with a hammer or small explosive charge. Many buildings in Iraq have such holes, and a new one does not attract much notice. *Harry Martinez, Shadow Team*

2005/02/05

The bullet hole in the windshield was produced by a shot from an insurgent sniper that hit an Iraqi army soldier in the back of the truck. Captain Charles Greene, a U.S. Army Ranger and adviser to Iraqi Special Forces, lined up the holes in the front and back windows, identified the enemy sniper's hide, and killed him as he attempted to take a second shot. *Charles Greene*

2005/01/28

Captain Charles Greene in his Iraqi Special Forces uniform and armed with the locally manufactured Tabuk sniper rifle. The Tabuk is based on the Yugoslav Zastava M70 and the 7.62x39mm cartridge (the same used in the AK-47) and is used extensively by both Iraqi military personnel and insurgents. It is considered effective to about six hundred meters. *Charles Greene*

2005/01/29

The Tabuk and similar weapons based on Warsaw Pact designs generally use a fixed four-power scope with integral rangefinding reticule. The calibrated line indicates the range to a standing man whose feet touch the lower horizontal line and whose head touches the curve. These children and the adult male at the left are at about 150 meters. *Charles Greene*

Right: Law-abiding Iraqis know better than to approach the dead or wounded on the street, and this woman and her child walk past the residue of a neighborhood brawl. Civil authorities will come along to pick up the body later. *Charles Greene*

Left: Ammunition for the M107 Barrett .50-caliber sniper weapon system tends to be very old manufacture, sometimes going back to the Korean War era and even before. But the rounds have been well preserved and normally function perfectly despite their age. **Middle:** Part of the issue of accuracy with the M107 has to do with the available ammunition, all of which is designed for use in variations of the M2 .50-caliber heavy machine gun, a weapon normally used to engage "area" targets. This magazine has been charged with both ball and tracer rounds. **Right:** Armor-piercing incendiary (API) ammunition is loaded in a ten-round magazine for the M107 Barrett. This is the traditional ammunition of choice when engaging vehicles like cars or trucks. Within a thousand meters or so it will punch a hole in an engine block or transmission. Hits on steel produce a bright flash from the incendiary filler.

The spotter and shooter work as a team to identify and engage specific targets as required by the instructors. These two students are part of the Sniper Leader Employment Course, a one-week program intended to help commanders properly utilize snipers within their command. The shooter is demonstrating poor position; he should be directly behind the gun, not off at an angle as he is here.

Staff Sergeant Timothy Johns has come from the 25th Infantry Division, stationed in Hawaii, to attend the course just before deployment to Iraq. He's flipping the bipod legs into position before taking his issued M107 to the firing line.

Sniper school concludes with an exhausting series of events and exercises at ranges and training areas in the Harmony Church area that are not graded but used to determine the Honor Student. Here comes Staff Sgt. Timothy Johns at a rapid Ranger pace, headed for the next event station.

The Barrett M107 has been very successful at its intended function—destroying hard targets like vehicles—for many years. An ingenious mechanism in the action and a very effective muzzle brake reduce felt recoil to approximately that of a 12-gauge shotgun.

The M107 adds about thirty pounds to the sniper's load, and that makes it a challenge to carry on missions that require long insertions, covert or otherwise. Teams normally break it down and split the load or trade off.

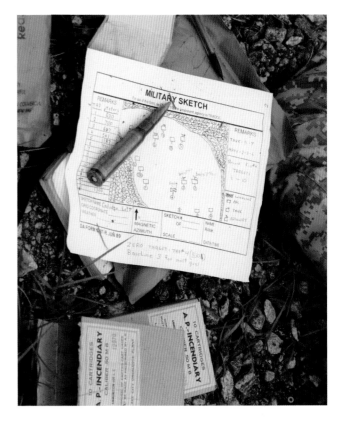

Before engaging targets with the M107, each student team has to develop a map of the firing area and the individual targets on the range. They will be instructed to engage targets by number, not description, and some shooters do poorly on the event when they fire and hit the wrong target.

A captain from the British army's Coldstream Guards lines up on his target at the Sixth Annual U.S. Army International Sniper Competition. The Barrett is in use with many armies around the world and has inspired several competitors. The Brits have had many years' experience with sniping in Northern Ireland and elsewhere and are frequent visitors to U.S. Army and Marine Corps sniper schools.

Inset: When the tactical situation requires snipers to fire multiple shots at the same time, the team leader calls "I have control, I have control, I have control." He then will normally count down from five, and the snipers fire on their targets at the same instant. The blue dump truck is filled with explosives in the back and dead bodies in the cab. Two snipers from Shadow Team made their kills through glass at 796 meters, a tough shot even without the barrier issue. *Harry Martinez, Shadow Team*

Above: The M107 Barrett is often used by snipers in urban hides and from positions unlike those taught in training programs. The tremendous muzzle blast of the weapon is bad enough outside, but special attention must be paid to wearing hearing protection when the rifle is fired in an enclosed space. This marine sniper is ready for targets during the battle of Fallujah. *U.S. Marine Corps, Lance Cpl. James J. Vooris*

Left: Ammunition used for training tends to be quite old, sometimes manufactured thirty or forty years ago, but most of it functions perfectly. Match-grade .50 caliber ammunition is available but has been in extremely short supply.

This sniper is ready to fire on targets from a UH-60 Blackhawk helicopter. Although the vibration of the helicopter makes accurate fire extremely difficult, there are some techniques that make it practical under certain conditions. One is to rig a strap or bungee cord to support the weapon while firing, and another is to fire from the prone position on a futon on the helicopter's deck, both techniques that will dampen the vibration somewhat.

Once snipers are in a combat area, they frequently test fire their weapons and confirm their sight alignment. This 3rd Infantry Division sniper is firing some rounds from his section's M107 at paper targets before taking it on a mission where it will fire on cars, trucks, and perhaps people. *Harry Martinez, Shadow Team*

When the occupants of this car were observed placing an IED in its trunk, they were marked for death. Two Shadow Team snipers executed a "volley fire" engagement on them, killing the driver first with a head shot and the other two members of the team with shots to the torso. When the vehicle was checked out, the trunk was found to contain weapons, ammunition, a large supply of cash, and an IED ready for emplacement. *Harry Martinez, Shadow Team*

TEN

The M24 sniper weapon system isn't normally supposed to be used for close-quarter combat, but the real world doesn't care what the manuals or the schools say.

Real-World Sniper Operations

The PVS-10 sight system is designed for both day and night use and is still in common issue although currently being replaced by superior hybrid systems. It is heavy at almost five pounds, bulky, and with a fixed 8.5-power optical system, is not as suitable for long-range engagements as variable-power scopes such as the Schmidt–Bender and Leupold Mk 4 types.

Learning to be a sniper in school and actually being a sniper in a combat zone are very different things. Once a sniper has been to one of the Marine Corps or army schools and has a Bravo Four ASI or 8541 MOS, the second phase of his education as a sniper begins.

Getting through the school does not automatically guarantee assignment to a sniper unit. Many graduates go back to their units and find themselves assigned to duties having nothing to do with the sniper mission. Some will go on to Ranger School or other training. The B4 additional skill identifier is, for some soldiers, just another ticket punch, just another qualification and school attended that will be considered when it is time for promotion.

Although snipers traditionally have not often needed frag grenades as part of their kit of tools of the trade, they need them now. Teams operating in urban environments are always at risk of ambushes and close-quarter combat, and these M67 frags get used fairly often. Sergeant Joseph Bennett from the 2nd Battalion, 69th Infantry, still has the pin from the one he used to kill two insurgents just outside the wall surrounding his team's Ramadi hide site.

It is up to the unit to decide how to employ its personnel, and most will consult the individual before assigning him to a slot. When the unit needs a sniper and a school-trained sniper shows up at the unit, he'll probably have a visit with the sniper section NCO, and after that perhaps an invitation to join the section.

Once assigned to the section, school-trained snipers can expect a probationary period during which they will be tested and evaluated by their peers and chain of command. One sniper section in Samarra, Iraq, put its new snipers through a grueling ordeal that involved dangerous and extremely physical nighttime covert insertions to hides. These insertions involved climbing up the sides of occupied buildings, jumping from one rooftop to another, clambering over high walls, and sneaking through occupied homes without being detected. Only after a satisfactory performance on these missions would this unit consider a school-trained sniper for a place on their section.

How sniper units actually work in combat varies somewhat and will have a lot to do with what tasks the snipers are assigned. Conventional force units normally assign snipers to a scout or recon platoon within the headquarters company. Snipers work for the battalion commander and report to his operations officer, or S3, for their missions. That means that these sniper sections are somewhat independent of the regular platoons and their regular chains of command. The sniper section

The M18 Claymore is a command-detonated mine that is normally fired electrically, normally when all hell is breaking loose. The weapon is issued in kit form, with everything you need in a handy little bag. There's one hundred feet of wire on a spool; an electrical cap already attached; the body of the mine, inside of which is plastic explosive and ball bearings; a circuit tester; and a little electrical generator that everybody calls a "clacker" because of its distinctive sound.

leader usually report to the ops officer and that puts the whole sniper team a lot closer to the battalion commander than all the other squad-sized units in the battalion. This can be a good or a bad thing, depending on how the battalion commander and his battle staff want to use their sniper element. For units that like snipers, their snipers can expect lots of missions and plenty of work. For units that don't care about using snipers, those snipers can expect to man an observation post in a tower or on a roof or to do similar mindnumbing assignments.

During week four, students learn about advanced ballistics and the problems of what is called "angle fire." When shooting at a target that is higher or lower than the shooter—at an enemy down in a valley, for example, when the sniper is on a ridge above—normal sight adjustments won't work. This device provides the shooter with a measurement of the angle to the target and, with the other usual ballistic data, may be used to calculate the "come-ups" to use for sight adjustment.

The Leupold Mk 3 day optic is a fixed ten-power scope with a mil-dot calibrated reticule, bullet-drop compensator, and adjustable focus. The scope is the foundation to precision delivery of fire, and it must be sturdy, waterproof, and hold its zero under combat conditions. Student snipers learn in week one to make sure the scope rings are torqued to sixty-five foot-pounds before every mission.

No, it is not an M16 but a 7.62mm rifle built around a modified version of the same design, the SR-25, manufactured by Knight's Armament. This weapon provides rapid reengagement times, a ten-round magazine, the same ballistics as the M24, and several other tactical advantages. Its reliability is considered less than any bolt gun like the M24, but many SEAL and other SOF sniper teams use the weapon successfully. This one is equipped with a sound suppressor.

Army and Marine Corps battalions do things a bit differently, but all conventional infantry units have a sniper section that has twelve to fifteen men assigned to it. A staff sergeant/E-6 normally leads the section, and he typically has three or four individual sniper teams. Each of these teams has two or three (and sometimes four) men assigned—one designated shooter, a designated spotter, plus one or two alternates who are trying out for the section or who are just along to provide additional security.

The senior man on each sniper team isn't the shooter but the spotter. The spotter has the most mission-critical job of identifying targets and calling shot impact, and those skills require more experience than accurate shot placement. The team leader's slot is an E-5 sergeant's rank. The shooter and other members of each team are usually E-4 specialists or corporals.

Not all the men in the sniper section are likely to be school-trained 8541s or B4s. SOP in most units is to recruit candidates for the section with the interest and aptitude to be snipers, then provide informal training to get each man ready to attend the school, and many may have been through this process prior to attendance at Fort Benning or Quantico or one of the other schools.

KILLING: THE SCHOOL SOLUTION VS. THE REAL WORLD

Today's sniper schools do a good job preparing their students for almost every aspect of the sniper mission, but there is one part of the job that can't be taught in school, and it is the most basic part of the job. That's the act of placing the cross hairs of the weapon sight on another human being and pulling the trigger that sends a bullet into somebody's head or chest and kills him. Despite all the psychological evaluations, all the lectures and the simulations on the range, soldiers and marines won't know if they are really snipers until the time

Each member of a team conducting a patrol or other tactical mission generally carries M18 smoke grenades. These grenades will put out a dense, bright smoke that can mark your position or screen you from enemy forces. But one thing about popping smoke—once you pull the pin on one, everybody knows exactly where you are!

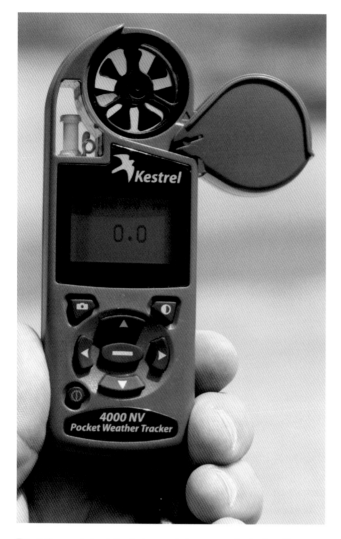

The major puzzle to delivering accurate long-range fire is the effect of wind on the projectile. Even a gentle breeze will shift the point of impact significantly at ranges over three hundred meters, and at eight hundred meters such a breeze can easily cause a miss. Wind velocity indicators like this Kestrel can tell you what the velocity is at the firing point, but students must learn to use clues downrange—the movement of trash in the street or laundry on clothes lines, grass, and leaves—to estimate how a bullet will be displaced on a long shot.

comes when a target presents itself, meets local rules of engagement, and they need to send a bullet downrange. If they had any doubts about their ability to make the shot, they shouldn't have signed up for sniper school—they would have been wasting everybody's time, especially their own. The essence of the sniper's mission is methodically and precisely killing people—usually men, sometimes women, and occasionally, in the worst situations, children.

Major Charles Greene, a Ranger sniper who was himself shot by an insurgent sniper, says, "There are three kinds of people who end up assigned to sniper teams. The first is the guy who, when the time comes, can't bring himself to pull the trigger and kill another person. The second type of person who comes out of sniper school and, when the time comes, pulls the trigger, makes a shot that kills a human being; this type of sniper becomes very remorseful, perhaps throws up and asks to be assigned to a different job. The third personality type we encounter is the guy who makes a kill, chambers a fresh round, starts scanning for new targets, and makes another kill as soon as he finds a target that meets ROE. This third personality type is the only one who belongs in sniper school but the only way to tell one of these types from the others is to put a man behind a gun and see if he's a killer, and if he'll kill again."

During the 1990s and into the 2000s, some sniper teams got very large numbers of confirmed kills in Iraq and Afghanistan. The most successful that the authors know about at this writing was Shadow Team from 2nd Battalion, 69th Infantry, 3rd Infantry Division (Mechanized). During one six-month period in 2005 and 2006, Shadow Team accumulated 276 confirmed kills, and several members of the ten-man unit made more than fifty kills each. Soldiers and marines shouldn't go to sniper school if they think they are unable to make that first kill, or the second, or the third. Their whole unit, and their unit's whole mission, may depend on their

The M107 rifle is only one part of a sniper's combat load, but a big and bulky one. Some teams disassemble the weapon and split it up for transport.

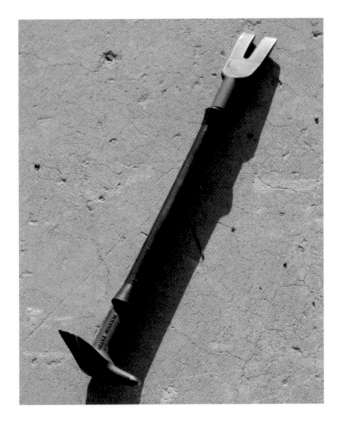

Dynamic-entry tools designed for SWAT teams have become standard equipment for some military sniper teams, especially those associated with special-operations units like SEALs, who do a lot of raids and forced entries.

ability to put a bullet in the head of a guy who is setting up an improvised explosive device (IED) or about to drop a mortar round down a tube. If they can't make kills, they should find a different job.

TOOLS OF THE TRADE—
SNIPER TEAM GEAR LOCKER

Once snipers get to a combat zone and a tactical unit conducting operations, all sorts of things are going to change. Their section will have its own little home away from home someplace within an FOB (forward operating base), and here they will have several large wall lockers where weapons and gear can be secured.

During their weeks in sniper school, they had lots of experience with the M40 and M24 sniper weapons systems, a day or two with the M107 Barrett, and a few hours training with the M9 Beretta pistol. When snipers get to a combat unit, they may find that the section does

Staff Sergeant Stan Crowder is one of those many die-hard combat snipers who just won't give up on the old ALICE-Large rucksack that has been an item of issue for about thirty years. On the right side of his ruck is an entrenching, or "E," tool, an excellent little folding shovel. Inside the ruck, Stan probably has everything he needs for a week in the field plus a mortar base-plate just to make the load a challenge.

a lot of things differently from the way the school taught, and uses different weapons as well.

Virtually all units have M24 or M40-series 7.62mm rifles essentially identical to those used at the schools. Unlike the school weapons, however, the shot-count on the barrels is likely to be lower and the groups these rifles shoot will be a bit tighter. Many of the tactical weapons will be configured to accept sound suppressors. They may have other modifications, too, such as an angle indicator attached to the scope. Especially in SOF units, after-market folding stocks may be used to make the weapon more compact during infiltration and extraction.

A sniper's weapons locker may have several rifles not used in school-house training, including the M21 or M14,

a 7.62mm semi-auto with twenty-round capacity, the SR-25, another 7.62mm rifle but with a ten-round capacity, M4 carbines or M16 rifles, and M9 Beretta pistols.

REAL-WORLD BATTLE RATTLE

When sniper students made stalks and infiltrations at school, they carried their M40 or M24 and a rucksack with some water, hide construction tools and materials, an MRE or two, perhaps a ghillie suit, a "deuce gear" or LBV, and not a lot more. This "battle rattle" added up to about thirty pounds, the rifle another twelve or so. Students thought this was all heavy and they thought Fort Benning was hot, but when they get to the "sandbox," they learn what *hot* and *heavy* really mean.

For starters, most units require snipers to wear full body armor during vehicle infiltration and extraction—helmet and "incapacitator" IBA with collar and shoulder extensions. While this armor will help protect from IED explosions, it is so heavy that moving in Iraq's furnace-like heat while wearing it causes many heat stress casualties. Most combat snipers report that they wear this level of protection only during infil and extract and leave it in the HMMWV when they move to their hide.

In the combat world, somebody on the team will have the primary radio, everybody will have spare batteries, and everybody might also carry little Motorola FRS radios for inter-team comms.

Nobody in school carries M4 or M16 rifles in addition to an M24 or M40, but SOP today is to keep the bolt gun in its bag during insertion and extraction while the M16 is carried locked and loaded in case of ambushes. Some units require each member of the sniper team to carry a full "basic load," seven 30-round magazines, one in the weapon's mag well, the other six in pouches on the sniper's load-bearing vest or body armor. Some units permit some of these mags to be carried in assault packs, others insist that they be on the LBV. The rated capacity of these seven 30-round mags is 210 rounds, but SOP for most units is to put only twenty-eight rounds in each magazine; stuffing them to full capacity results in more "stoppages."

Everybody in most real-world units carries grenades—M67 frags and M18 smokes. They weigh about a pound each and add to the load. Further adding to the load, in some units and on some missions, will be M18 Claymore command-detonated mines and blocks of C4 explosive, plus blasting caps, time fuse, fuse lighters, and det cord. These blasting materials are often preformed and primed for use to breach doors and walls but can be used in a pinch as improvised grenades. These materials are, of course, extremely dangerous and most soldiers and marines don't train with them much until they arrive in a combat zone. This makes them even more dangerous. Both grenades and explosives are useful tools with special handling requirements. When snipers end up in a combat zone and in a unit that issues them, they should get additional training if they can—they should be comfortable with explosives, never complacent.

Depending on the mission, a sniper might be carrying eight or more liters of water. Some guys like to use canteens, others prefer CamelBaks or HydraStorm hydration bladders, but plain bottled water in two-liter containers solves the problem just as well. The ancient one-quart canteen that has been issued to American soldiers and marines for more than one hundred years is still in the supply system but has been largely displaced by water bottles made of almost unbreakable Lexan. These new water bottles were developed by the rock-climbing and mountaineering recreation industry and adopted by military personnel. The wide-mouth versions are often favored because they are easy to fill and can be used to mix soups and other dried mixes.

When empty, the commercial throwaway water bottles have another use—guys can pee in them. There are no working bathrooms in most sniper hides and snipers don't want to leave anything in the place to indicate that it has been used—especially human waste—to alert the enemy about the use of the location because snipers might want to use it again. Teams normally bring empty bottles and plastic bags for sanitary cleanup.

Snipers bring along a combination tool—Leatherman, Gerber, SOG, or one of the other brands—to cut wire, attach

Another technique that is sometimes effective against enemy snipers is to use a dummy or outline of a torso, usually with clothing attached, in an effort to get the enemy to take a shot. When he does, an American sniper team will be watching and waiting. These are members of 1st Battalion, 8th Marines. *USMC*

Opposite: Counter-sniper operations are among the most important for snipers, and many techniques have been used to lure the enemy out to where he can be killed. Here a member of 1st Battalion, 8th Marines, tries to lure insurgents to show their position by firing on a helmet extended out over a wall and into the open during Operation Al Fajr. *USMC, Lance Cpl. J. A. Chaverri*

Snipers have to use what is available when threats and targets present themselves. The Leupold Mk 3 scope is a handicap for situations like this, with targets at fifty meters, but that is not stopping this sniper from engaging with his M24 sniper weapon system.

antennas, open flex-cuffs, and a million other little chores. Sniper missions typically last many hours and sometimes several days, so snipers normally consider what kind of food to bring along. MREs are typically "field-stripped" down to the only components snipers really expect to use, shaving an ounce or two from each one. Many guys prefer a Ziploc bag of trail mix, jerky, cheese and crackers, or similar snack items that aren't likely to melt in the heat.

Snipers won't leave home without a few pounds of signaling devices—a recognition panel, chem-lights, signal mirror, M2000 strobe, and perhaps an infrared laser target designator. And a mission packing list won't be complete without at least one GPS system, an issued precision lightweight GPS receiver (PLGR, or "plugger")

or one of the many civilian versions. Many soldiers buy their own (Magellan's Etrex seems to be the most popular) because they are quite inexpensive, much lighter and less bulky than the PLGR, and are practically as accurate. Soldiers aren't supposed to use them for certain tactical needs such as calling for air or artillery support, but they get used that way anyway.

REAL-WORLD TACTICS, TECHNIQUES, AND PROCEDURES

The way actual combat sniper missions are planned and executed varies tremendously from one unit to another, from one day to another. Well-trusted sniper sections are often given great latitude in planning and executing their missions. They are allowed to pick their area of

Specialist Francesco Musso, a sniper with Headquarters and Headquarters Company, 2nd Battalion, 35th Infantry Regiment, 25th Infantry Division, pulls security in Qalat, Afghanistan, October 9, 2004. The patrol was checking voting places during the Afghanistan presidential election. *U.S. Army, Staff Sgt. Joseph P. Collins, Jr. (Released)*

operations and may determine when and how they will operate. Missions for these units can be quite casual, entirely planned and coordinated by the members of the sniper section itself.

Other units and other kinds of missions begin with a "warning order" and subsequent operations orders issued by the command staff. For these missions, the sniper section is often just a bit player in a larger play, providing support while the battalion's maneuver elements execute a cordon-and-search or a patrol or a raid.

Mission planning can be very detailed and thorough. It can involve overhead imagery, intel reports from confidential sources and telephone intercepts, plus information from dozens of reports from a wide variety of sources. Mission planning considers the risks and the rewards of the proposed action, the resources necessary

Specialist Ross Henderson of the Mortar Platoon, 2nd Battalion, 27th Infantry, 25th Infantry Division, Schofield Barracks, Hawaii, watches out for possible enemy forces while at a halt during a convoy to the Gayan District of Afghanistan on October 7, 2004. The soldiers are members of a platoon that will provide support and security for the Afghan National Army during the October 9, 2004, Afghanistan elections. The soldiers of this platoon deployed to Afghanistan in support of Operation Enduring Freedom. *U.S. Army, Spc. Jerry T. Combes*

to make it successful, and the coordination required to keep everybody on the same proverbial "sheet of music."

Remember all the time the snipers spent working on their ghillie suits in school? Well, it will stay in their locker when they get deployed to Iraq or Afghanistan. They're going to have to learn a whole new set of stalking and hide-site building skills for current combat operations.

For example, there is the problem of all the watch dogs; people in Muslim nations don't keep dogs as pets, they keep them for guard purposes. The local breeds are almost wild animals and their barking alerts the locals to a sniper's presence. "The first thing you need to do," one sniper says of missions in rural Iraq, "is to kill all the dogs where you are going to operate. Get a .22-caliber pistol with a sound suppressor on it and shoot them in the head."

Sniper school trains students to make deliberate, individual, precision shots with M24s and M40s at long range, more than 600 meters away. Real-world engagements today are much more often at shorter ranges, often less than 100 meters, and involve multiple targets that must be rapidly killed. Instead of bolt guns, many teams are using their "rack grade" or specially prepared M16s to make their kills. Fort Benning's Army Marksmanship Unit's gunsmiths have been upgrading M16s with heavier barrels, two-stage match triggers, and optical sights that are extremely popular with snipers in urban terrain. When fed 77-grain Black Hills ammunition, this combination is deadly out to 700 meters and the weapon of choice on many teams.

HUNTING IED EMPLACEMENT TEAMS

Extremely common and often productive missions in Iraq involve the ones against IED emplacement teams. These enemy teams have their own SOPs and are very

Introduction to the M24 Sniper Weapon System

In 1988, the U.S. Army adopted the M24 sniper weapon system, replacing the M21 that dated to 1969. The M21 was a modified M14 semi-automatic rifle and the adoption of the M24 was a return to bolt-action sniper rifles by the U.S. Army. Like the Marine Corps' sniper rifle, the M40, the M21 is based on the Remington 700. The M24 sniper rifle is a five-shot, bolt-action repeating rifle capable of engaging targets out to 800 meters, although it can successfully engage targets out to 1,000 meters depending on the shooter. The preferred ammunition for the M24 is the NATO 7.62mm M118 Long Range, which fires a match grade 175-grain projectile. The length of the weapon is 43 inches, with the stock fully collapsed, and it weighs, with five rounds, sling, and the day sight optics, 4.25 pounds. The entire M24 sniper weapon system weighs sixty-four pounds and consists of more than just the rifle. It includes:

- The M24 sniper rifle
- System hard case
- Soft case
- M1907 sling
- Iron sight/day sight optic case
- TM 9-1005-306-10
- Deployment kit
- Optional Harris bipod

The M24 rifle has six component groups: the receiver, trigger assembly, stock, barrel, bolt, and sighting systems.

The receiver is a Remington 700, long-action receiver. The reason for the long action is so the weapon may be converted to fire the .300 Winchester Magnum if necessary. There is a five-shot internal magazine attached to the lower portion of the receiver. The safety is located at the right rear of the receiver, behind the bolt handle.

The trigger assembly has a trigger with a pull that is adjustable from 2 to 8 pounds. The hex-head screw on the face of the trigger is for adjusting the weight of pull. Turning the screw to the right increases trigger weight; turning the screw to the left decreases trigger weight. The bolt stop release is located in front of the base of the trigger. The floor plate release is located outside on the front of the trigger guard.

The stock is made of Kevlar reinforced fiberglass material. The primary advantage of a synthetic stock is that humidity has a lesser effect than it does on a wooden stock. Synthetic stocks are more rugged and do not age like their wooden counterparts. This stock uses an aluminum-bedding block to seat the receiver in the stock for a perfect fit. The aluminum-bedding block gives the rifle better consistency and accuracy.

The stainless steel barrel is 24 inches long and has five radials with one turn in 11.2 inches. For enhanced accuracy the barrel is free floating, which means that no portion of the barrel touches the stock from the receiver to the muzzle.

The bolt is a long-action bolt with a user replaceable firing pin. Each bolt is individually tuned for each rifle and is therefore non-interchangeable with bolts for other M24s. The last four digits of the receiver's serial number is printed on the bottom of the bolt handle to avoid installing the wrong bolt in the wrong rifle.

The M24 may be used with three sighting systems: a day optic sight, a day/night optic sight, and iron sights. The primary sighting system is the Leupold M3A Ultra telescope. It has a fixed magnification of 10 power, fully coated lenses, mil dot reticle, and a bullet drop compensator (BDC) designed for the M118 special ball/long range cartridge. The M24 may also be used with the AN/PVS 10, an integrated day/night scope that can provide both day and night firing capability in a single sight. Finally, the M24 is provided with match quality Redfield Palma iron sights for use in the event that the primary optics are damaged.

A scout sniper with Headquarters Company, 3rd Battalion, 5th Marine Regiment, 1st Marine Division, scans for insurgents in the streets and buildings along the edge of Fallujah, Iraq, during the first hours of Operation Al Fajr, November 8, 2004. *USMC, Lance Cpl. James J. Vooris*

sophisticated about how, where, and when they emplace their weapons. Sniper teams have learned to spot these enemy teams and have their own SOPs for dealing with them.

A very large proportion of sniper missions and kills are against these enemy teams, and these missions are very much unlike those for which the schools train. These engagements are typically at close range, often less than 100 meters, and often involve multiple targets that must be engaged almost simultaneously. The M24 and M40 bolt-action sniper rifles are not designed for such engagements and are too slow for effective reengagement when cover and concealment for enemy targets are available.

As a result, those M16 and M4 rifles, often tricked out with PEQ-4 laser sighting systems and sound suppressors, have been getting a lot of the kills made by sniper teams. As mentioned elsewhere, 3rd Infantry Division's Shadow Team has been spectacularly successful in

Ramadi with their M107 Barretts, M24s, but especially with their M16s. Shadow destroyed an IED emplacement team on its very first mission, all the kills made with M16s from a distance of only 65 meters. Staff Sergeant Harry Martinez, a 28th Infantry Division National Guardsman "chopped" to Shadow, killed three enemy insurgents with his M16 on his first mission, also at close range.

Some sniper SOPs and TTPs (tactics, techniques, and procedures) must remain secret and won't be discussed here, but some are common knowledge among the enemy. One is that, in an ambush on multiple enemy personnel in a vehicle, the driver always dies first. That makes it more difficult for the rest of the team to escape. Another is that the ambush won't be initiated until all the personnel are back in their vehicle, with the doors closed. That makes them proverbial fish in the proverbial barrel.

140

A U.S. Marine attached to 1st Battalion, 8th Marine Regiment, 1st Marine Division, looks for insurgent activity in Fallujah, Iraq, November 10, 2004, during Operation Al Fajr. *USMC, Lance Cpl. Trevor R. Gift*

INDEX

Other Zenith Press titles of interest to the enthusiast:

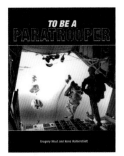

To Be a Paratrooper
978-0-7603-3046-3

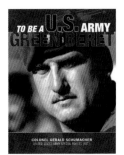

To Be a U.S. Army Green Beret
978-0-7603-2107-2

Night Stalkers
978-0-7603-2141-6

Mafia Allies
978-0-7603-2457-8

Tales from a Tin Can
978-0-7603-2770-8

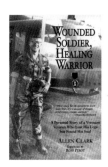

Wounded Soldier, Healing Warrior
978-0-7603-3113-2

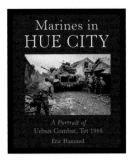

Marines in Hue City
978-0-7603-2521-6

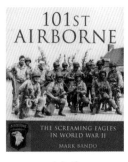

101st Airborne
978-0-7603-2984-9

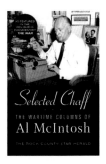

Selected Chaff
978-0-7603-3355-6